# Standards Practice Book

For Home or School
Grade 2

**INCLUDES:**
- Home or School Practice
- Lesson Practice and Test Preparation
- English and Spanish School-Home Letters
- Getting Ready for Grade 3 Lessons

Copyright © by Houghton Mifflin Harcourt Publishing Company.

All rights reserved. No part of this work may be reproduced or transmitted in any form or by any means, electronic or mechanical, including photocopying or recording, or by any information storage and retrieval system, without the prior written permission of the copyright owner unless such copying is expressly permitted by federal copyright law. Requests for permission to make copies of any part of the work should be addressed to Houghton Mifflin Harcourt Publishing Company, Attn: Contracts, Copyrights, and Licensing, 9400 South Park Center Loop, Orlando, Florida 32819.

Common Core State Standards © Copyright 2010. National Governors Association Center for Best Practices and Council of Chief State School Officers. All rights reserved.

This product is not sponsored or endorsed by the Common Core State Standards Initiative of the National Governors Association Center for Best Practices and the Council of Chief State School Officers.

Printed in the U.S.A.

ISBN 978-0-547-58814-8

30  0928  20

4500803101            D E F G

If you have received these materials as examination copies free of charge, Houghton Mifflin Harcourt Publishing Company retains title to the materials and they may not be resold. Resale of examination copies is strictly prohibited.

Possession of this publication in print format does not entitle users to convert this publication, or any portion of it, into electronic format.

# Number Sense and Place Value

**Critical Area** Extending understanding of base-ten notation

## 1 Number Concepts

**Domains** Operations and Algebraic Thinking
Number and Operations in Base Ten
**Common Core Standards** CC.2.OA.3, CC.2.NBT.2, CC.2.NBT.3

|  |  |  |
|---|---|---|
|  | School-Home Letter (English) . . . . . . . . . . . . . . . . . . . . . . . . . . . | **P1** |
|  | School-Home Letter (Spanish) . . . . . . . . . . . . . . . . . . . . . . . . . . | **P2** |
| 1.1 | **Hands On:** Algebra • Even and Odd Numbers . . . . . . . . . . . . | **P3** |
| 1.2 | **Algebra** • Represent Even Numbers. . . . . . . . . . . . . . . . . . . . . | **P5** |
| 1.3 | Understand Place Value . . . . . . . . . . . . . . . . . . . . . . . . . . . . . | **P7** |
| 1.4 | Expanded Form. . . . . . . . . . . . . . . . . . . . . . . . . . . . . . . . . . . . | **P9** |
| 1.5 | Different Ways to Write Numbers . . . . . . . . . . . . . . . . . . . . . . | **P11** |
| 1.6 | **Algebra** • Different Names for Numbers . . . . . . . . . . . . . . . . | **P13** |
| 1.7 | **Problem Solving** • Tens and Ones . . . . . . . . . . . . . . . . . . . . . | **P15** |
| 1.8 | Counting Patterns Within 100 . . . . . . . . . . . . . . . . . . . . . . . . . | **P17** |
| 1.9 | Counting Patterns Within 1,000 . . . . . . . . . . . . . . . . . . . . . . . | **P19** |
|  | Extra Practice. . . . . . . . . . . . . . . . . . . . . . . . . . . . . . . . . . . . . . | **P21** |

## 2 Numbers to 1,000

**Domains** Number and Operations in Base Ten
**Common Core Standards** CC.2.NBT.1, CC.2.NBT.1a, CC.2.NBT.1b, CC.2.NBT.3, CC.2.NBT.4, CC.2.NBT.8

|  |  |  |
|---|---|---|
|  | School-Home Letter (English) . . . . . . . . . . . . . . . . . . . . . . . . . . | **P23** |
|  | School-Home Letter (Spanish) . . . . . . . . . . . . . . . . . . . . . . . . . | **P24** |
| 2.1 | Group Tens as Hundreds . . . . . . . . . . . . . . . . . . . . . . . . . . . . . | **P25** |
| 2.2 | Explore 3-Digit Numbers . . . . . . . . . . . . . . . . . . . . . . . . . . . . . | **P27** |
| 2.3 | **Hands On** • Model 3-Digit Numbers . . . . . . . . . . . . . . . . . . . | **P29** |
| 2.4 | Hundreds, Tens, and Ones . . . . . . . . . . . . . . . . . . . . . . . . . . . | **P31** |
| 2.5 | Place Value to 1,000 . . . . . . . . . . . . . . . . . . . . . . . . . . . . . . . . | **P33** |
| 2.6 | Number Names . . . . . . . . . . . . . . . . . . . . . . . . . . . . . . . . . . . . | **P35** |
| 2.7 | Different Forms of Numbers . . . . . . . . . . . . . . . . . . . . . . . . . . | **P37** |
| 2.8 | **Algebra** • Different Ways to Show Numbers. . . . . . . . . . . . . . | **P39** |
| 2.9 | Count On and Count Back by 10 and 100 . . . . . . . . . . . . . . . | **P41** |
| 2.10 | **Algebra** • Number Patterns . . . . . . . . . . . . . . . . . . . . . . . . . . | **P43** |
| 2.11 | **Problem Solving** • Compare Numbers . . . . . . . . . . . . . . . . . . | **P45** |
| 2.12 | **Algebra** • Compare Numbers . . . . . . . . . . . . . . . . . . . . . . . . . | **P47** |
|  | Extra Practice. . . . . . . . . . . . . . . . . . . . . . . . . . . . . . . . . . . . . . | **P49** |

# CRITICAL AREA: Addition and Subtraction

**COMMON CORE** **Critical Area** Building fluency with addition and subtraction

## 3 Basic Facts and Relationships

**Domains** Operations and Algebraic Thinking
**Common Core Standards** CC.2.OA.1, CC.2.OA.2, CC.2.OA.4

| | | |
|---|---|---|
| | School-Home Letter (English) | P51 |
| | School-Home Letter (Spanish) | P52 |
| 3.1 | Use Doubles Facts | P53 |
| 3.2 | Practice Addition Facts | P55 |
| 3.3 | **Algebra** • Make a Ten to Add | P57 |
| 3.4 | **Algebra** • Add 3 Addends | P59 |
| 3.5 | **Algebra** • Relate Addition and Subtraction | P61 |
| 3.6 | Practice Subtraction Facts | P63 |
| 3.7 | Use Ten to Subtract | P65 |
| 3.8 | **Algebra** • Use Drawings to Represent Problems | P67 |
| 3.9 | **Algebra** • Use Equations to Represent Problems | P69 |
| 3.10 | **Problem Solving** • Equal Groups | P71 |
| 3.11 | **Algebra** • Repeated Addition | P73 |
| | Extra Practice | P75 |

## 4 2-Digit Addition

**Domains** Operations and Algebraic Thinking
Number and Operations in Base Ten
**Common Core Standards** CC.2.OA.1, CC.2.NBT.5, CC.2.NBT.6, CC.2.NBT.9

| | | |
|---|---|---|
| | School-Home Letter (English) | P77 |
| | School-Home Letter (Spanish) | P78 |
| 4.1 | Break Apart Ones to Add | P79 |
| 4.2 | Use Compensation | P81 |
| 4.3 | Break Apart Addends as Tens and Ones | P83 |
| 4.4 | Model Regrouping for Addition | P85 |
| 4.5 | Model and Record 2-Digit Addition | P87 |
| 4.6 | 2-Digit Addition | P89 |
| 4.7 | Practice 2-Digit Addition | P91 |
| 4.8 | Rewrite 2-Digit Addition | P93 |
| 4.9 | **Problem Solving** • Addition | P95 |
| 4.10 | **Algebra** • Write Equations to Represent Addition | P97 |

| 4.11 | **Algebra** • Find Sums for 3 Addends | P99 |
| 4.12 | **Algebra** • Find Sums for 4 Addends | P101 |
| | Extra Practice | P103 |

## 5  2-Digit Subtraction

**Domains** Operations and Algebraic Thinking
Number and Operations in Base Ten
**Common Core Standards** CC.2.OA.1, CC.2.NBT.5, CC.2.NBT.9

| | School-Home Letter (English) | P105 |
| | School-Home Letter (Spanish) | P106 |
| 5.1 | **Algebra** • Break Apart Ones to Subtract | P107 |
| 5.2 | **Algebra** • Break Apart Numbers to Subtract | P109 |
| 5.3 | Model Regrouping for Subtraction | P111 |
| 5.4 | Model and Record 2-Digit Subtraction | P113 |
| 5.5 | 2-Digit Subtraction | P115 |
| 5.6 | Practice 2-Digit Subtraction | P117 |
| 5.7 | Rewrite 2-Digit Subtraction | P119 |
| 5.8 | Add to Find Differences | P121 |
| 5.9 | **Problem Solving** • Subtraction | P123 |
| 5.10 | **Algebra** • Write Equations to Represent Subtraction | P125 |
| 5.11 | Solve Multistep Problems | P127 |
| | Extra Practice | P129 |

## 6  3-Digit Addition and Subtraction

**Domains** Number and Operations in Base Ten
**Common Core Standards** CC.2.NBT.7

| | School-Home Letter (English) | P131 |
| | School-Home Letter (Spanish) | P132 |
| 6.1 | Draw to Represent 3-Digit Addition | P133 |
| 6.2 | Break Apart 3-Digit Addends | P135 |
| 6.3 | **3-Digit Addition:** Regroup Ones | P137 |
| 6.4 | **3-Digit Addition:** Regroup Tens | P139 |
| 6.5 | **Addition:** Regroup Ones and Tens | P141 |
| 6.6 | **Problem Solving** • 3-Digit Subtraction | P143 |
| 6.7 | **3-Digit Subtraction:** Regroup Tens | P145 |
| 6.8 | **3-Digit Subtraction:** Regroup Hundreds | P147 |
| 6.9 | **Subtraction:** Regroup Hundreds and Tens | P149 |
| 6.10 | Regrouping with Zeros | P151 |
| | Extra Practice | P153 |

# CRITICAL AREA: Measurement and Data

**COMMON CORE** **Critical Area** Using standard units of measure

## 7 Money and Time
**Domains** Measurement and Data
**Common Core Standards** CC.2.MD.7, CC.2.MD.8

| | | |
|---|---|---|
| | School-Home Letter (English) | P155 |
| | School-Home Letter (Spanish) | P156 |
| 7.1 | Dimes, Nickels, and Pennies | P157 |
| 7.2 | Quarters | P159 |
| 7.3 | Count Collections | P161 |
| 7.4 | **Hands On** • Show Amounts in Two Ways | P163 |
| 7.5 | One Dollar | P165 |
| 7.6 | Amounts Greater Than $1 | P167 |
| 7.7 | **Problem Solving** • Money | P169 |
| 7.8 | Time to the Hour and Half Hour | P171 |
| 7.9 | Time to 5 Minutes | P173 |
| 7.10 | Practice Telling Time | P175 |
| 7.11 | A.M. and P.M. | P177 |
| | Extra Practice | P179 |

## 8 Length in Customary Units
**Domains** Measurement and Data
**Common Core Standards** CC.2.MD.1, CC.2.MD.2, CC.2.MD.3, CC.2.MD.5, CC.2.MD.6, CC.2.MD.9

| | | |
|---|---|---|
| | School-Home Letter (English) | P181 |
| | School-Home Letter (Spanish) | P182 |
| 8.1 | **Hands On** • Measure With Inch Models | P183 |
| 8.2 | **Hands On** • Make and Use a Ruler | P185 |
| 8.3 | Estimate Lengths in Inches | P187 |
| 8.4 | **Hands On** • Measure with an Inch Ruler | P189 |
| 8.5 | **Problem Solving** • Add and Subtract in Inches | P191 |
| 8.6 | **Hands On** • Measure in Inches and Feet | P193 |
| 8.7 | Estimate Lengths in Feet | P195 |
| 8.8 | Choose a Tool | P197 |
| 8.9 | Display Measurement Data | P199 |
| | Extra Practice | P201 |

## 9 Length in Metric Units

**Domains** Measurement and Data
**Common Core Standards** CC.2.MD.1, CC.2.MD.2, CC.2.MD.3, CC.2.MD.4, CC.2.MD.5, CC.2.MD.6

|  | School-Home Letter (English) . . . . . . . . . . . . . . . . . . . . . . P203 |
|---|---|
|  | School-Home Letter (Spanish) . . . . . . . . . . . . . . . . . . . . . . P204 |
| 9.1 | **Hands On** • Measure with a Centimeter Model . . . . . . . . . . . . P205 |
| 9.2 | Estimate Lengths in Centimeters . . . . . . . . . . . . . . . . . . . . P207 |
| 9.3 | **Hands On** • Measure with a Centimeter Ruler . . . . . . . . . . . . P209 |
| 9.4 | **Problem Solving** • Add and Subtract Lengths . . . . . . . . . . . . P211 |
| 9.5 | **Hands On** • Centimeters and Meters . . . . . . . . . . . . . . . . . . P213 |
| 9.6 | Estimate Lengths in Meters . . . . . . . . . . . . . . . . . . . . . . . . P215 |
| 9.7 | **Hands On** • Measure and Compare Lengths . . . . . . . . . . . . . P217 |
|  | Extra Practice . . . . . . . . . . . . . . . . . . . . . . . . . . . . . . . . . P219 |

## 10 Data

**Domains** Measurement and Data
**Common Core Standards** CC.2.MD.10

|  | School-Home Letter (English) . . . . . . . . . . . . . . . . . . . . . . P221 |
|---|---|
|  | School-Home Letter (Spanish) . . . . . . . . . . . . . . . . . . . . . . P222 |
| 10.1 | Collect Data . . . . . . . . . . . . . . . . . . . . . . . . . . . . . . . . . P223 |
| 10.2 | Read Picture Graphs . . . . . . . . . . . . . . . . . . . . . . . . . . . . P225 |
| 10.3 | Make Picture Graphs . . . . . . . . . . . . . . . . . . . . . . . . . . . P227 |
| 10.4 | Read Bar Graphs . . . . . . . . . . . . . . . . . . . . . . . . . . . . . . P229 |
| 10.5 | Make Bar Graphs . . . . . . . . . . . . . . . . . . . . . . . . . . . . . . P231 |
| 10.6 | **Problem Solving** • Display Data . . . . . . . . . . . . . . . . . . . . P233 |
|  | Extra Practice . . . . . . . . . . . . . . . . . . . . . . . . . . . . . . . . . P235 |

# Geometry and Fractions

 **Critical Area** Describing and analyzing shapes

## 11  Geometry and Fraction Concepts

**Domains** Geometry
**Common Core Standards** CC.2.G.1, CC.2.G.2, CC.2.G.3

|  | |  |
|---|---|---|
|  | School-Home Letter (English) | P237 |
|  | School-Home Letter (Spanish) | P238 |
| 11.1 | Three-Dimensional Shapes | P239 |
| 11.2 | Attributes of Three-Dimensional Shapes | P241 |
| 11.3 | Two-Dimensional Shapes | P243 |
| 11.4 | Angles in Two-Dimensional Shapes | P245 |
| 11.5 | Sort Two-Dimensional Shapes | P247 |
| 11.6 | **Hands On** • Partition Rectangles | P249 |
| 11.7 | Equal Parts | P251 |
| 11.8 | Show Equal Parts of a Whole | P253 |
| 11.9 | Describe Equal Parts | P255 |
| 11.10 | **Problem Solving** • Equal Shares | P257 |
|  | Extra Practice | P259 |

# End-of-Year Resources

## Getting Ready for Grade 3

These lessons review important skills and prepare you for Grade 3.

| | | |
|---|---|---|
| **Lesson 1** | Find Sums on an Addition Table | P261 |
| **Lesson 2** | **Estimate Sums:** 2-Digit Addition | P263 |
| **Lesson 3** | **Estimate Sums:** 3-Digit Addition | P265 |
| **Lesson 4** | **Estimate Differences:** 2-Digit Subtraction | P267 |
| **Lesson 5** | **Estimate Differences:** 3-Digit Subtraction | P269 |
| **Lesson 6** | Order 3-Digit Numbers | P271 |
| **Checkpoint** | | P273 |
| **Lesson 7** | Equal Groups of 2 | P275 |
| **Lesson 8** | Equal Groups of 5 | P277 |
| **Lesson 9** | Equal Groups of 10 | P279 |
| **Lesson 10** | **Hands On:** Size of Shares | P281 |
| **Lesson 11** | **Hands On:** Number of Equal Shares | P283 |
| **Lesson 12** | Solve Problems with Equal Shares | P285 |
| **Checkpoint** | | P287 |
| **Lesson 13** | Hour Before and Hour After | P289 |
| **Lesson 14** | Elapsed Time in Hours | P291 |
| **Lesson 15** | Elapsed Time in Minutes | P293 |
| **Lesson 16** | **Hands On:** Capacity • Nonstandard Units | P295 |
| **Lesson 17** | Describe Measurement Data | P297 |
| **Checkpoint** | | P299 |
| **Lesson 18** | **Fraction Models:** Thirds and Sixths | P301 |
| **Lesson 19** | **Fraction Models:** Fourths and Eighths | P303 |
| **Lesson 20** | Compare Fraction Models | P305 |
| **Checkpoint** | | P307 |

# Chapter 1

# School-Home Letter

## Dear Family,

My class started Chapter 1 this week. In this chapter, I will learn about place value of 2-digit numbers and even and odd numbers.

Love, _____

## Vocabulary

**digits** 0, 1, 2, 3, 4, 5, 6, 7, 8, and 9 are digits.

**even numbers** 2, 4, 6, 8, 10 . . .

**odd numbers** 1, 3, 5, 7, 9 . . .

## Home Activity

Give your child a group of 20 small objects, such as beans. Have your child count the objects and tell how many. Then have your child pair the objects and tell whether the number is *even* or *odd*. Repeat with a different number of beans.

## Literature

Look for this book at the library. Ask your child to point out math vocabulary words as you read the book together.

**One Hundred Hungry Ants** by Elinor J. Pinczes. Houghton Mifflin, 1993.

# Capítulo 1

## Carta para la casa

### Querida familia:

Mi clase comenzó el Capítulo 1 esta semana. En este capítulo, aprenderé sobre el valor posicional de los números de 2 dígitos y números pares e impares.

Con cariño, _____

### Vocabulario

**dígitos** 0, 1, 2, 3, 4, 5, 6, 7, 8 y 9 son dígitos.

**números pares** 2, 4, 6, 8, 10 . . .

**números impares** 1, 3, 5, 7, 9 . . .

### Actividad para la casa

Dé a su hijo un grupo de 20 objetos pequeños, como unos frijoles. Pídale que cuente los objetos y que diga cuántos hay. Luego, pídale que los agrupe y diga si el número es *par* o *impar*. Repita con un número distinto de frijoles.

### Literatura

Busque este libro en la biblioteca. Pídale a su hijo que señale palabras del vocabulario de matemáticas mientras leen juntos el libro.

**One Hundred Hungry Ants**
por Elinor J. Pinczes.
Houghton Mifflin, 1993.

Name _____

# Algebra • Even and Odd Numbers

**HANDS ON
Lesson 1.1**

**COMMON CORE STANDARD** CC.2.OA.3
Work with equal groups of objects to gain foundations for multiplication.

Shade in the ten frames to show the number. Circle even or odd.

1. 15

even    odd

2. 18

even    odd

3. 11

even    odd

4. 17

even    odd

5. 13

even    odd

6. 20

even    odd

## PROBLEM SOLVING REAL WORLD

7. Mr. Dell has an odd number of sheep and an even number of cows on his farm. Circle the choice that could tell about his farm.

9 sheep and 10 cows

10 sheep and 11 cows

8 sheep and 12 cows

Chapter 1    three **P3**

# Lesson Check (CC.2.OA.3)

1. Which of these numbers is an even number?
   - ○ 3
   - ○ 4
   - ○ 5
   - ○ 9

2. Which of these numbers is an odd number?
   - ○ 2
   - ○ 6
   - ○ 7
   - ○ 8

# Spiral Review (CC.2.OA.3)

3. Which of these numbers is an odd number? (Lesson 1.1)
   - ○ 10
   - ○ 8
   - ○ 3
   - ○ 4

4. Which of these numbers is an even number? (Lesson 1.1)
   - ○ 7
   - ○ 6
   - ○ 5
   - ○ 1

5. Which of these numbers is an even number? (Lesson 1.1)
   - ○ 9
   - ○ 7
   - ○ 5
   - ○ 2

6. Which of these numbers is an odd number? (Lesson 1.1)
   - ○ 1
   - ○ 4
   - ○ 8
   - ○ 10

P4 four

Name _____

# Algebra • Represent Even Numbers

**Lesson 1.2**

**COMMON CORE STANDARD CC.2.OA.3**
Work with equal groups of objects to gain foundations for multiplication.

Shade in the frames to show two equal groups for each number. Complete the addition sentence to show the groups.

1. 8      __ = __ + __

2. 18    __ = __ + __

3. 10    __ = __ + __

4. 14    __ = __ + __

5. 20    __ = __ + __

6. 12    __ = __ + __

## PROBLEM SOLVING  REAL WORLD

Solve. Write or draw to explain.

7. The seats in a van are in pairs. There are 16 seats. How many pairs of seats are there?

_____ pairs of seats

Chapter 1          five **P5**

## Lesson Check (CC.2.OA.3)

1. Which sum is an even number?
   - ○ 9 + 9 = 18
   - ○ 9 + 8 = 17
   - ○ 8 + 7 = 15
   - ○ 6 + 5 = 11

2. Which sum is an even number?
   - ○ 1 + 2 = 3
   - ○ 3 + 3 = 6
   - ○ 2 + 5 = 7
   - ○ 4 + 7 = 11

## Spiral Review (CC.2.OA.3)

3. Which is an even number?
   
   (Lesson 1.1)
   - ○ 7
   - ○ 9
   - ○ 10
   - ○ 13

4. Which is an odd number?
   
   (Lesson 1.1)
   - ○ 4
   - ○ 11
   - ○ 16
   - ○ 20

5. Ray has an odd number of cats. He also has an even number of dogs. Which can be Ray's pets?
   
   (Lesson 1.1)
   - ○ 3 cats and 1 dog
   - ○ 3 cats and 3 dogs
   - ○ 4 cats and 2 dogs
   - ○ 5 cats and 2 dogs

6. Which sum is an even number?
   
   (Lesson 1.2)
   - ○ 2 + 3 = 5
   - ○ 3 + 4 = 7
   - ○ 4 + 4 = 8
   - ○ 7 + 8 = 15

Name _____

**Understand Place Value**

Lesson 1.3

COMMON CORE STANDARD CC.2.NBT.3
Understand place value.

**Circle the value of the underlined digit.**

1.  2<u>3</u>

    20    2

2.  <u>4</u>8

    8    80

3.  1<u>8</u>

    10    1

4.  <u>4</u>3

    40    4

5.  <u>5</u>4

    5    50

6.  <u>6</u>5

    50    5

7.  <u>7</u>0

    7    70

8.  3<u>7</u>

    70    7

9.  <u>2</u>2

    20    2

## PROBLEM SOLVING

Write the 2-digit number that matches the clues.

10. My number has a tens digit that is 8 more than the ones digit. Zero is not one of my digits.

My number is _____.

Chapter 1          seven **P7**

# Lesson Check (CC.2.NBT.3)

1. What is the value of the underlined digit?

   3<u>2</u>

   ○ 2      ○ 20
   ○ 3      ○ 30

2. What is the value of the underlined digit?

   <u>2</u>8

   ○ 80      ○ 8
   ○ 20      ○ 2

# Spiral Review (CC.2.OA.3, CC.2.NBT.3)

3. What is the value of the underlined digit? (Lesson 1.3)

   <u>5</u>3

   ○ 50      ○ 8
   ○ 30      ○ 5

4. What is the value of the underlined digit? (Lesson 1.3)

   2<u>4</u>

   ○ 40      ○ 6
   ○ 20      ○ 4

5. Which of these choices is an even number of pens and an odd number of pencils? (Lesson 1.1)

   ○ 7 pens 7 pencils
   ○ 5 pens 4 pencils
   ○ 2 pens 3 pencils
   ○ 2 pens 2 pencils

6. Which sum is an even number? (Lesson 1.2)

   ○ 5 + 2 = 7
   ○ 6 + 3 = 9
   ○ 7 + 4 = 11
   ○ 7 + 7 = 14

Name _____

# Expanded Form

**Lesson 1.4**

COMMON CORE STANDARD CC.2.NBT.3
Understand place value.

**Draw a quick picture to show the number. Describe the number in two ways.**

1. 68

    ____ tens ____ ones

    ____ + ____

2. 21

    ____ tens ____ one

    ____ + ____

3. 70

    ____ tens ____ ones

    ____ + ____

4. 53

    ____ tens ____ ones

    ____ + ____

5. 35

    ____ tens ____ ones

    ____ + ____

6. 47

    ____ tens ____ ones

    ____ + ____

## PROBLEM SOLVING

7. Circle the ways to write the number shown by the model.

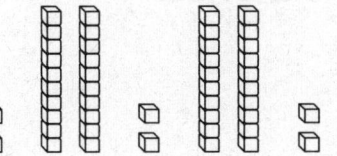

    4 tens 6 ones    40 + 6    64

    6 tens 4 ones    60 + 4    46

Chapter 1      nine **P9**

# Lesson Check (CC.2.NBT.3)

1. Which is a way to describe the number 92?
   - ○ 9 tens
   - ○ 2 tens 9 ones
   - ○ 9 tens 2 ones
   - ○ 11 tens

2. Which is a way to describe the number 45?
   - ○ 4 tens 5 ones
   - ○ 5 tens 4 ones
   - ○ 4 tens 0 ones
   - ○ 4 tens 9 ones

# Spiral Review (CC.2.NBT.3)

3. What is the value of the underlined digit? (Lesson 1.3)

   4<u>9</u>

   - ○ 90
   - ○ 40
   - ○ 9
   - ○ 4

4. What is the value of the underlined digit? (Lesson 1.3)

   3<u>4</u>

   - ○ 40
   - ○ 30
   - ○ 4
   - ○ 3

5. Which is another way to describe the number 76?
   (Lesson 1.4)

   - ○ 7 tens
   - ○ 6 tens 7 ones
   - ○ 7 tens 6 ones
   - ○ 7 tens 13 ones

6. Which is another way to describe the number 52?
   (Lesson 1.4)

   - ○ 7 tens 2 ones
   - ○ 2 tens 5 ones
   - ○ 5 tens
   - ○ 5 tens 2 ones

Name _____

# Different Ways to Write Numbers

**Lesson 1.5**

COMMON CORE STANDARD CC.2.NBT.3
Understand place value.

**Write the number another way.**

1. 32

   ____ tens ____ ones

2. forty-one

   _____

3. 9 tens 5 ones

   _____

4. 80 + 3

   _____

5. 57

   ____ tens ____ ones

6. seventy-two

   ____ + ____

7. 60 + 4

   _____

8. 4 tens 8 ones

   _____

9. twenty-eight

   ____ + ____

10. 80

    ____ tens ____ ones

## PROBLEM SOLVING

11. A number has the digit 3 in the ones place and the digit 4 in the tens place. Which of these is another way to write this number? Circle it.

    3 + 4      40 + 3      30 + 4

Chapter 1

eleven **P11**

## Lesson Check (CC.2.NBT.3)

1. Which is another way to write 3 tens 9 ones?
   - ○ 93
   - ○ 30 + 90
   - ○ 90 + 3
   - ○ 39

2. Which is another way to write the number eighteen?
   - ○ 8 + 1
   - ○ 81
   - ○ 10 + 8
   - ○ 10 + 80

## Spiral Review (CC.2.NBT.3)

3. Which is another way to write the number 47? (Lesson 1.5)
   - ○ 70 + 4
   - ○ 40 + 7
   - ○ 4 + 7
   - ○ 40 + 70

4. Which is another way to write the number 95? (Lesson 1.5)
   - ○ 50 + 9
   - ○ 90 + 50
   - ○ fifty-nine
   - ○ ninety-five

5. What is the value of the underlined digit? (Lesson 1.3)

   6<u>1</u>

   - ○ 1
   - ○ 6
   - ○ 7
   - ○ 10

6. What is the value of the underlined digit? (Lesson 1.3)

   <u>1</u>7

   - ○ 1
   - ○ 7
   - ○ 10
   - ○ 70

P12 twelve

Name _____

# Algebra • Different Names for Numbers

**Lesson 1.6**

COMMON CORE STANDARD CC.2.NBT.3
Understand place value.

The blocks show the number in different ways.
Describe the blocks in two ways.

1. 24

____ tens ____ ones
____ + ____

____ ten ____ ones
____ + ____

____ tens ____ ones
____ + ____

2. 36

____ tens ____ ones
____ + ____

____ ten ____ ones
____ + ____

____ tens ____ ones
____ + ____

3. 45

____ tens ____ ones
____ + ____

____ tens ____ ones
____ + ____

____ tens ____ ones
____ + ____

## PROBLEM SOLVING REAL WORLD

4. Toni has these blocks. Circle the blocks that she could use to show 34.

Chapter 1     thirteen **P13**

# Lesson Check (CC.2.NBT.3)

1. What number is shown with the blocks?

   2 tens 13 ones

   ○ 33
   ○ 34
   ○ 43
   ○ 63

2. What number is shown with the blocks?

   1 ten 16 ones

   ○ 16
   ○ 26
   ○ 31
   ○ 36

# Spiral Review (CC.2.NBT.3)

3. What number is shown with the blocks? (Lesson 1.6)

   1 ten 17 ones

   ○ 17     ○ 27
   ○ 42     ○ 57

4. What is the value of the underlined digit? (Lesson 1.3)

   2<u>9</u>

   ○ 2      ○ 20
   ○ 9      ○ 90

5. Which is another way to write 9 tens 3 ones? (Lesson 1.5)

   ○ 39
   ○ 30 + 9
   ○ 90
   ○ 93

6. How many tens and ones are in the number 50? (Lesson 1.4)

   ○ 0 tens 5 ones
   ○ 2 tens 3 ones
   ○ 5 tens 0 ones
   ○ 5 tens 5 ones

# Problem Solving • Tens and Ones

**PROBLEM SOLVING**
**Lesson 1.7**

COMMON CORE STANDARD CC.2.NBT.3
Understand place value.

**Find a pattern to solve.**

1. Ann is grouping 38 rocks. She can put them into groups of 10 rocks or as single rocks. What are the different ways Ann can group the rocks?

| Groups of 10 rocks | Single rocks |
|---|---|
|  |  |
|  |  |
|  |  |
|  |  |

2. Mr. Grant needs 30 pieces of felt. He can buy them in packs of 10 or as single pieces. What are the different ways Mr. Grant can buy the felt?

| Packs of 10 pieces | Single pieces |
|---|---|
|  |  |
|  |  |
|  |  |
|  |  |

3. Ms. Sims is putting away 22 books. She can put them on the table in stacks of 10 or as single books. What are the different ways Ms. Sims can put away the books?

| Stacks of 10 books | Single books |
|---|---|
|  |  |
|  |  |
|  |  |

Chapter 1

# Lesson Check (CC.2.NBT.3)

1. Mrs. Chang is packing 38 apples. She can pack them in bags of 10 or as single apples. What choice is missing from the list of ways Mrs. Chang can pack the apples?

   ○ 3 bags, 0 single apples
   ○ 1 bag, 18 single apples
   ○ 3 bags, 8 single apples
   ○ 4 bags, 8 single apples

| Bags of 10 apples | Single apples |
|---|---|
| 2 | 18 |
| 1 | 28 |
| 0 | 38 |

# Spiral Review (CC.2.NBT.3)

2. What is the value of the underlined digit? (Lesson 1.3)

   <u>5</u>4

   ○ 50
   ○ 40
   ○ 5
   ○ 4

3. What number is shown with the blocks? (Lesson 1.6)

   2 tens 19 ones

   ○ 21
   ○ 29
   ○ 34
   ○ 39

4. Which is another way to write the number 62? (Lesson 1.5)

   ○ 2 tens 6 ones
   ○ 20 + 6
   ○ sixty-two
   ○ 60 + 20

5. What number can be written as 8 tens 6 ones? (Lesson 1.5)

   ○ 68
   ○ 86
   ○ 114
   ○ 140

Name _____

## Counting Patterns Within 100

**Lesson 1.8**

COMMON CORE STANDARD CC.2.NBT.2
Understand place value.

**Count by ones.**

1. 58, 59, ____, ____, ____, ____, ____

**Count by fives.**

2. 45, 50, ____, ____, ____, ____, ____

3. 20, 25, ____, ____, ____, ____, ____

**Count by tens.**

4. 20, ____, ____, ____, ____, ____, ____

**Count back by ones.**

5. 87, 86, 85, ____, ____, ____

### PROBLEM SOLVING REAL WORLD

6. Tim counts his friends' fingers by fives.
   He counts the fingers on six hands.
   What numbers does he say?

   5, ____, ____, ____, ____, ____

Chapter 1      seventeen **P17**

## Lesson Check (CC.2.NBT.2)

1. Which group of numbers shows counting by fives?
   ○ 17, 18, 19, 20, 21
   ○ 70, 75, 80, 85, 90
   ○ 20, 30, 40, 50, 60
   ○ 65, 64, 63, 62, 61

2. Which group of numbers shows counting by tens?
   ○ 10, 11, 12, 13, 14
   ○ 20, 25, 30, 35, 40
   ○ 60, 70, 80, 90, 100
   ○ 10, 9, 8, 7, 6

## Spiral Review (CC.2.OA.3, CC.2.NBT.2, CC.2.NBT.3)

3. Which group of numbers shows counting back by ones? (Lesson 1.8)
   ○ 21, 20, 19, 18, 17
   ○ 25, 30, 35, 40, 45
   ○ 88, 89, 90, 91, 92
   ○ 30, 40, 50, 60, 70

4. A number is shown with 2 tens and 15 ones. Which of these is a way to write the number?
   (Lesson 1.6)
   ○ fifteen          ○ twenty
   ○ twenty-five   ○ thirty-five

5. Which of these is another way to describe 72? (Lesson 1.4)
   ○ 70 + 20
   ○ 70 + 2
   ○ 20 + 7
   ○ 7 + 2

6. What sum is an even number?
   (Lesson 1.2)
   ○ 2 + 5 = 7
   ○ 3 + 6 = 9
   ○ 9 + 9 = 18
   ○ 5 + 6 = 11

P18 eighteen

Name _____

# Counting Patterns Within 1,000

**Lesson 1.9**

COMMON CORE STANDARD CC.2.NBT.2
Understand place value.

**Count by fives.**

1. 415, 420, _____, _____, _____, _____

2. 675, 680, _____, _____, _____, _____, _____

**Count by tens.**

3. 210, 220, _____, _____, _____, _____, _____

4. 840, 850, _____, _____, _____, _____, _____

**Count by hundreds.**

5. 300, 400, _____, _____, _____, _____, _____

**Count back by ones.**

6. 953, 952, _____, _____, _____, _____, _____

## PROBLEM SOLVING REAL WORLD

7. Lee has a jar of 100 pennies.
She adds groups of 10 pennies to the jar.
She adds 5 groups. What numbers does she say?

_____, _____, _____, _____, _____

Chapter 1

# Lesson Check (CC.2.NBT.2)

1. Which group of numbers shows counting by tens?
   - ○ 875, 870, 865, 860, 855
   - ○ 191, 192, 193, 194, 195
   - ○ 160, 170, 180, 190, 200
   - ○ 115, 120, 125, 130, 145

2. Which group of numbers shows counting by hundreds?
   - ○ 850, 860, 870, 880, 890
   - ○ 620, 625, 630, 635, 640
   - ○ 150, 149, 148, 147, 146
   - ○ 400, 500, 600, 700, 800

# Spiral Review (CC.2.NBT.2, CC.2.NBT.3)

3. Which group of numbers shows counting by fives? (Lesson 1.9)
   - ○ 245, 250, 255, 260, 265
   - ○ 105, 104, 103, 102, 101
   - ○ 355, 455, 555, 655, 755
   - ○ 550, 560, 570, 580, 590

4. Which group of numbers shows counting back by ones? (Lesson 1.8)
   - ○ 17, 18, 19, 20, 21
   - ○ 71, 70, 69, 68, 67
   - ○ 25, 20, 15, 10, 5
   - ○ 40, 50, 60, 70, 80

5. Which is another way to describe 45? (Lesson 1.4)
   - ○ 45 tens 0 ones
   - ○ 9 tens 5 ones
   - ○ 5 tens 4 ones
   - ○ 4 tens 5 ones

6. Which is another way to write 7 tens 9 ones? (Lesson 1.5)
   - ○ ninety-seven
   - ○ eighty-nine
   - ○ 79
   - ○ 16

Name _____

COMMON CORE STANDARDS CC.2.OA.3,
CC.2.NBT.2, CC.2.NBT.3

# Chapter 1 Extra Practice

**Lesson 1.1** (pp. 13–16) . . . . . . . . . . . . . . . . . . . . . . . . . . . . . . . . . . . . . . . . . . .
Shade in the ten frames to show the number.
Circle **even** or **odd**.

1. 17

2. 20

even    odd

even    odd

**Lesson 1.3** (pp. 21–24) . . . . . . . . . . . . . . . . . . . . . . . . . . . . . . . . . . . . . . . . . . .
Circle the value of the underlined digit.

1. 5<u>7</u>

70        7

2. <u>9</u>3

90        9

**Lesson 1.4** (pp. 25–28) . . . . . . . . . . . . . . . . . . . . . . . . . . . . . . . . . . . . . . . . . . .
Draw a quick picture to show the number.
Describe the number in two ways.

1. 22

2. 67

____ tens ____ ones

____ + ____

____ tens ____ ones

____ + ____

Chapter 1

twenty-one  **P21**

# Lesson 1.6 (pp. 33–36)

The blocks show the numbers in different ways.
Describe the blocks in two ways.

1. 48

____ tens ____ ones          ____ tens ____ ones          ____ tens ____ ones

____ + ____                  ____ + ____                  ____ + ____

# Lesson 1.7 (pp. 37–40)

Find a pattern to solve.

1. Jack baked 38 biscuits. He can store them in boxes of 10 biscuits or as single biscuits. What are all of the different ways Jack can store the biscuits?

| Boxes of 10 biscuits | Single biscuits |
|---|---|
|  |  |
|  |  |
|  |  |
|  |  |

# Lessons 1.8 - 1.9 (pp. 41–48)

Count by tens.

1. 50, _____, _____, _____, _____, _____

Count back by ones.

2. 37, 36, 35, 34, _____, _____, _____

Count by fives.

3. 455, 460, _____, _____, _____, _____, _____

Count by hundreds.

4. 100, 200, _____, _____, _____, _____, _____

P22   twenty-two

# Chapter 2 School-Home Letter

## Dear Family,

My class started Chapter 2 this week. I will learn about place value of numbers to 1,000. I will also learn about comparing these numbers.

Love, _____

## Vocabulary

**compare** To describe whether numbers are equal to, less than, or greater than one another

**hundred** A group of 10 tens

**is equal to** 145 is equal to 145

**=** 145 = 145

**is greater than** 131 is greater than 121

**>** 131 > 121

**is less than** 125 is less than 185

**<** 125 < 185

**thousand** A group of 10 hundreds

## Home Activity

Have your child look through magazines for 3-digit numbers and cut them out. Work together to write a word problem using two of these numbers, gluing the cut-out numbers in place. Have your child solve the problem.

Charles collected __127__ leaves. Ann collected __240__ leaves. Who collected the greater number of leaves?

## Literature

Reading math stories reinforces learning. Look for these books in the library.

**A Place for Zero**
by Angeline Sparagna LoPresti and Phyllis Hornung. Charlesbridge Publishing, 2003.

**More or Less**
by Stuart J. Murphy. HarperCollins, 2005.

Chapter 2     twenty-three **P23**

# Capítulo 2

# Carta para la casa

## Querida familia:

Mi clase comenzó el Capítulo 2 esta semana. Aprenderé sobre el valor posicional de los números hasta 1,000. También aprenderé a comparar estos números.

Con cariño, _____

## Vocabulario

**comparar** Describir si los números son iguales a, menores que o mayores que otro número

**centena** Un grupo de 10 decenas

**es igual a** 145 es igual a 145

**=** 145 = 145

**es mayor que** 131 es mayor que 121

**>** 131 > 121

**es menor que** 125 es menor que 185

**<** 125 < 185

**millar** Un grupo de 10 centenas

## Actividad para la casa

Pídale a su hijo que busque números de 3 dígitos en revistas y que los recorte. Luego, trabajen juntos para escribir un problema usando dos de estos números y péguenlos en algún lugar. Pídale a su hijo que resuelva el problema.

Carlos juntó __127__ hojas.
Ana juntó __240__ hojas.
¿Quién juntó el mayor número de hojas?

## Literatura

Leer cuentos de matemáticas refuerza el aprendizaje. Busque estos libros en la biblioteca.

**A Place for Zero**
por Angeline Sparagna LoPresti and Phyllis Hornung.
Charlesbridge Publishing, 2003.

**More or Less**
por Stuart J. Murphy
HarperCollins, 2005.

P24 twenty-four

Name _____

**Lesson 2.1**

## Group Tens as Hundreds

COMMON CORE STANDARDS CC.2.NBT.1a, CC.2.NBT.1b
Understand place value.

Write how many tens. Circle groups of 10 tens.
Write how many hundreds. Write the number.

1. _____ tens
   _____ hundreds
   _____

2. _____ tens
   _____ hundreds
   _____

3. _____ tens
   _____ hundreds
   _____

**PROBLEM SOLVING**

Solve. Write or draw to explain.

4. Farmer Gray has 30 flowerpots.
   He plants 10 seeds in each pot.
   How many seeds does he plant?

   _____ seeds

Chapter 2 twenty-five **P25**

## Lesson Check (CC.2.NBT.1a, CC.2.NBT.1b)

1. Which number has the same value as 40 tens?
   - ○ 4010
   - ○ 400
   - ○ 40
   - ○ 4

2. Which number has the same value as 80 tens?
   - ○ 8
   - ○ 80
   - ○ 800
   - ○ 8010

## Spiral Review (CC.2.OA.3, CC.2.NBT.2, CC.2.NBT.3)

3. Which of these is a way to show the number 63? (Lesson 1.6)
   - ○ 5 tens 13 ones
   - ○ 5 tens 3 ones
   - ○ 3 tens 6 ones
   - ○ 1 ten 63 ones

4. Which group of numbers shows counting by fives? (Lesson 1.8)
   - ○ 5, 6, 7, 8, 9
   - ○ 5, 10, 15, 20, 25
   - ○ 50, 60, 70, 80, 90
   - ○ 50, 51, 52, 53, 54

5. Carlos has 58 pencils. What is the value of the digit 5 in this number? (Lesson 1.3)
   - ○ 5
   - ○ 8
   - ○ 13
   - ○ 50

6. Which sum is an even number? (Lesson 1.2)
   - ○ 2 + 3 = 5
   - ○ 4 + 4 = 8
   - ○ 5 + 6 = 11
   - ○ 8 + 7 = 15

P26 twenty-six

Name _____

# Explore 3-Digit Numbers

**Lesson 2.2**

COMMON CORE STANDARD CC.2.NBT.1
Understand place value.

**Circle tens to make 1 hundred. Write the number in different ways.**

1. _____ tens
   _____ hundred _____ tens

2. _____ tens
   _____ hundred _____ tens

3. _____ tens
   _____ hundred _____ tens

## PROBLEM SOLVING

Solve. Write or draw to explain.

4. Millie has a box of 1 hundred cubes. She also has a bag of 70 cubes. How many trains of 10 cubes can she make?

   _____ trains of 10 cubes

Chapter 2     twenty-seven **P27**

# Lesson Check (CC.2.NBT.1)

1. Which has the same value as 12 tens?

   - ○ 2 hundreds 2 tens
   - ○ 1 hundred 2 tens
   - ○ 2 tens 1 one
   - ○ 1 ten 2 ones

2. Which has the same value as 15 tens?

   - ○ 1 ten 5 ones
   - ○ 5 tens 1 one
   - ○ 1 hundred 5 tens
   - ○ 5 hundreds 1 ten

# Spiral Review (CC.2.OA.3, CC.2.NBT.3)

3. Which of these is an odd number? (Lesson 1.1)
   - ○ 18
   - ○ 10
   - ○ 9
   - ○ 4

4. Which of these is a way to show the number 35? (Lesson 1.6)
   - ○ 2 tens 15 ones
   - ○ 3 tens 0 ones
   - ○ 3 tens 15 ones
   - ○ 5 tens 3 ones

5. Which of these is another way to describe 78? (Lesson 1.4)
   - ○ 7 + 8
   - ○ 70 + 8
   - ○ 70 + 80
   - ○ 80 + 7

6. Which is another way to write the number 55? (Lesson 1.5)
   - ○ 15 + 5
   - ○ 25
   - ○ fifty
   - ○ 5 tens 5 ones

Name _____

# Model 3-Digit Numbers

**HANDS ON
Lesson 2.3**

**COMMON CORE STANDARD** CC.2.NBT.1
Understand place value.

Write how many hundreds, tens, and ones.
Show with ▨ ▭ .. Then draw a quick picture.

1. 118

| Hundreds | Tens | Ones |
|----------|------|------|
|          |      |      |

2. 246

| Hundreds | Tens | Ones |
|----------|------|------|
|          |      |      |

3. 143

| Hundreds | Tens | Ones |
|----------|------|------|
|          |      |      |

4. 237

| Hundreds | Tens | Ones |
|----------|------|------|
|          |      |      |

## PROBLEM SOLVING

5. Write the number that matches the clues.

   • My number has 2 hundreds.
   • The tens digit is 9 more than the ones digit.

   My number is _____.

| Hundreds | Tens | Ones |
|----------|------|------|
|          |      |      |

Chapter 2

twenty-nine **P29**

# Lesson Check (CC.2.NBT.1)

1. What number is shown with these blocks?

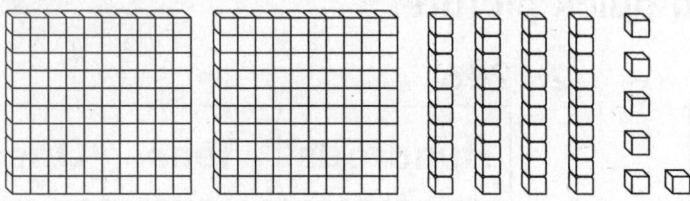

| Hundreds | Tens | Ones |
|---|---|---|
|  |  |  |

246   264   462   642
○     ○     ○     ○

# Spiral Review (CC.2.OA.3, CC.2.NBT.1a, CC.2.NBT.1b, CC.2.NBT.3)

2. Which number has the same value as 28 tens? (Lesson 2.1)
   - ○ 28
   - ○ 280
   - ○ 2800
   - ○ 2810

3. Which of these is another way to describe 59? (Lesson 1.4)
   - ○ 90 + 50
   - ○ 90 + 5
   - ○ 50 + 9
   - ○ 5 + 9

4. Which of these is an odd number? (Lesson 1.1)
   - ○ 11
   - ○ 12
   - ○ 18
   - ○ 20

5. Which of these is a way to show the number 73? (Lesson 1.6)
   - ○ 3 tens 7 ones
   - ○ 7 tens 3 ones
   - ○ 30 tens 7 ones
   - ○ 70 tens 3 ones

Name _____

# Hundreds, Tens, and Ones

**Lesson 2.4**

COMMON CORE STANDARD CC.2.NBT.1
Understand place value.

Write how many hundreds, tens, and ones are in the model. Write the number in two ways.

1.

| Hundreds | Tens | Ones |
|----------|------|------|
|          |      |      |

_____

_____ + _____ + _____

2.

| Hundreds | Tens | Ones |
|----------|------|------|
|          |      |      |

_____

_____ + _____ + _____

3.

| Hundreds | Tens | Ones |
|----------|------|------|
|          |      |      |

_____

_____ + _____ + _____

## PROBLEM SOLVING

4. Write the number that answers the riddle. Use the chart.
A model for my number has 6 ones blocks, 2 hundreds blocks, and 3 tens blocks.
What number am I?

| Hundreds | Tens | Ones |
|----------|------|------|
|          |      |      |

_____

Chapter 2                                                thirty-one  **P31**

# Lesson Check (CC.2.NBT.1)

1. Which is a way to write the number 254?

   ○ 200 + 50 + 4
   ○ 400 + 20 + 5
   ○ 400 + 50 + 2
   ○ 500 + 40 + 3

2. Which is a way to write the number 307?

   ○ 700 + 30 + 0
   ○ 300 + 0 + 7
   ○ 30 + 70 + 0
   ○ 0 + 3 + 7

# Spiral Review (CC.2.OA.3, CC.2.NBT.1a, CC.2.NBT.1b, CC.2.NBT.3)

3. Which of these is another way to describe 83? (Lesson 1.4)

   ○ 8 + 3
   ○ 8 + 30
   ○ 80 + 3
   ○ 80 + 30

4. Which is another way to write 86? (Lesson 1.5)

   ○ 806
   ○ eighty-six
   ○ 6 tens 8 ones
   ○ 8 + 6

5. Which number has the same value as 32 tens? (Lesson 2.1)

   ○ 32
   ○ 320
   ○ 3200
   ○ 3210

6. Which of these is an odd number? (Lesson 1.1)

   ○ 2
   ○ 6
   ○ 10
   ○ 17

P32 thirty-two

Name _____

## Place Value to 1,000

**Lesson 2.5**

COMMON CORE STANDARD CC.2.NBT.1
Understand place value.

**Circle the value or the meaning of the underlined digit.**

| | | | |
|---|---|---|---|
| 1. 3<u>3</u>7 | 3 | 30 | 300 |
| 2. 46<u>2</u> | 200 | 20 | 2 |
| 3. <u>5</u>72 | 5 | 50 | 500 |
| 4. 56<u>7</u> | 7 ones | 7 tens | 7 hundreds |
| 5. <u>4</u>62 | 4 hundreds | 4 ones | 4 tens |
| 6. <u>1</u>,000 | 1 ten | 1 hundred | 1 thousand |

## PROBLEM SOLVING

7. Write the 3-digit number that answers the riddle.

 • I have the same hundreds digit as ones digit.

 • The value of my tens digit is 50.

 • The value of my ones digit is 4.    The number is _____.

Chapter 2

thirty-three **P33**

# Lesson Check (CC.2.NBT.1)

1. What is the value of the underlined digit?

    3̲15

    ○ 3
    ○ 30
    ○ 33
    ○ 300

2. What is the meaning of the underlined digit?

    64̲8

    ○ 4 ones
    ○ 4 tens
    ○ 4 hundreds
    ○ 4 thousands

# Spiral Review (CC.2.OA.3, CC.2.NBT.1, CC.2.NBT.3)

3. Which number can be written as 40 + 5? (Lesson 1.4)

    ○ 4
    ○ 9
    ○ 45
    ○ 54

4. Which number has the same value as 14 tens? (Lesson 2.2)

    ○ 140
    ○ 104
    ○ 40
    ○ 14

5. Which of these is a way to show the number 26? (Lesson 1.6)

    ○ 6 tens 2 ones
    ○ 2 tens 2 ones
    ○ 1 ten 16 ones
    ○ 1 ten 6 ones

6. Which of these is an even number? (Lesson 1.1)

    ○ 7
    ○ 16
    ○ 21
    ○ 25

P34 thirty-four

Name _____

## Number Names

**Lesson 2.6**

**COMMON CORE STANDARD** CC.2.NBT.3
Understand place value.

**Write the number.**

1. two hundred thirty-two

   _____

2. five hundred forty-four

   _____

3. one hundred fifty-eight

   _____

4. nine hundred fifty

   _____

5. four hundred twenty

   _____

6. six hundred seventy-eight

   _____

**Write the number using words.**

7. 317

   _____

8. 457

   _____

### PROBLEM SOLVING REAL WORLD

Circle the answer.

9. Six hundred twenty-six children attend Elm Street School. Which is another way to write this number?

   266    626    662

Chapter 2

thirty-five **P35**

## Lesson Check (CC.2.NBT.3)

1. Which is another way to write the number 851?

   ○ one hundred fifty-eight
   ○ five hundred eighteen
   ○ five hundred eighty-one
   ○ eight hundred fifty-one

2. Which is another way to write the number two hundred sixty?

   ○ 206
   ○ 216
   ○ 260
   ○ 266

## Spiral Review (CC.2.NBT.1, CC.2.NBT.2)

3. Which of these numbers has the digit 8 in the tens place? (Lesson 2.5)

   ○ 280
   ○ 468
   ○ 508
   ○ 819

4. What number is shown with these blocks? (Lesson 2.3)

   ○ 209     ○ 425
   ○ 245     ○ 542

5. Which group of numbers shows counting by fives? (Lesson 1.9)

   ○ 650, 655, 660, 665
   ○ 555, 655, 755, 855
   ○ 550, 560, 570, 580
   ○ 540, 541, 542, 543

6. Sam has 128 marbles. How many hundreds are in this number? (Lesson 2.4)

   ○ 110
   ○ 100
   ○ 10
   ○ 1

Name _____

## Different Forms of Numbers

**Lesson 2.7**

**COMMON CORE STANDARD** CC.2.NBT.3
Understand place value.

Read the number and draw a quick picture.
Then write the number in different ways.

1. two hundred fifty-one

   ____ hundreds ____ tens ____ one

   _____ + _____ + _____

   _____

2. three hundred twelve

   ____ hundreds ____ ten ____ ones

   _____ + _____ + _____

   _____

3. two hundred seven

   ____ hundreds ____ tens ____ ones

   _____ + _____ + _____

   _____

## PROBLEM SOLVING

Write the number another way.

4. 200 + 30 + 7

   _____

5. 895

   _____

Chapter 2

thirty-seven **P37**

# Lesson Check (CC.2.NBT.3)

1. Which is another way to write the number 392?
   - ○ 300 + 90 + 2
   - ○ 300 + 19 + 2
   - ○ 200 + 90 + 3
   - ○ 200 + 30 + 9

2. Which is another way to write the number 271?
   - ○ 1 hundred 7 tens 2 ones
   - ○ 2 hundreds 1 ten 7 ones
   - ○ 2 hundreds 2 tens 7 ones
   - ○ 2 hundreds 7 tens 1 one

# Spiral Review (CC.2.NBT.1, CC.2.NBT.3)

3. What is the value of the underlined digit? (Lesson 1.3)

   5<u>6</u>
   - ○ 5
   - ○ 6
   - ○ 50
   - ○ 60

4. What number is shown with these blocks? (Lesson 2.3)

   - ○ 221
   - ○ 212
   - ○ 210
   - ○ 122

5. Which is another way to write the number 75? (Lesson 1.5)
   - ○ 705
   - ○ 70 + 5
   - ○ seventy-one
   - ○ 5 tens 7 ones

6. Which number can be written as 60 + 3? (Lesson 1.4)
   - ○ 6
   - ○ 9
   - ○ 36
   - ○ 63

Name _____

# Algebra • Different Ways to Show Numbers

Lesson **2.8**

**COMMON CORE STANDARD CC.2.NBT.3**
Understand place value.

Write how many hundreds, tens, and ones are in the model.

1. 135

| Hundreds | Tens | Ones |
|---|---|---|
|  |  |  |

| Hundreds | Tens | Ones |
|---|---|---|
|  |  |  |

2. 216

| Hundreds | Tens | Ones |
|---|---|---|
|  |  |  |

| Hundreds | Tens | Ones |
|---|---|---|
|  |  |  |

## PROBLEM SOLVING REAL WORLD

Markers are sold in boxes, packs, or as single markers. Each box has 10 packs. Each pack has 10 markers.

3. Draw pictures to show two ways to buy 276 markers.

Chapter 2          thirty-nine **P39**

# Lesson Check (CC.2.NBT.3)

1. Which of the following numbers can be shown with this many hundreds, tens, and ones?

| Hundreds | Tens | Ones |
|---|---|---|
| 1 | 2 | 18 |

- ○ 128
- ○ 129
- ○ 138
- ○ 148

2. Which of the following numbers can be shown with this many hundreds, tens, and ones?

| Hundreds | Tens | Ones |
|---|---|---|
| 2 | 15 | 6 |

- ○ 256
- ○ 266
- ○ 316
- ○ 356

# Spiral Review (CC.2.NBT.3)

3. Which number can be written as 6 tens 2 ones? (Lesson 1.6)

- ○ 26
- ○ 62
- ○ 206
- ○ 602

4. Which number can be written as 30 + 2? (Lesson 1.4)

- ○ 302
- ○ 203
- ○ 32
- ○ 23

5. Which is another way to write the number 584? (Lesson 2.7)

- ○ five hundred eighty-four
- ○ 500 + 8 + 4
- ○ five hundred eighteen
- ○ 50 + 80 + 4

6. Which is another way to write the number 29? (Lesson 1.5)

- ○ 209
- ○ 9 tens 2 ones
- ○ 90 + 2
- ○ twenty-nine

Name _____

## Count On and Count Back by 10 and 100

**Lesson 2.9**

**COMMON CORE STANDARD** CC.2.NBT.8
Use place value understanding and properties of operations to add and subtract.

**Write the number.**

1. 10 more than 451
   _____

2. 10 less than 770
   _____

3. 100 more than 367
   _____

4. 100 less than 895
   _____

5. 10 less than 812
   _____

6. 100 more than 543
   _____

7. 10 more than 218
   _____

8. 100 more than 379
   _____

9. 100 less than 324
   _____

10. 10 less than 829
    _____

## PROBLEM SOLVING

Solve. Write or draw to explain.

11. Sarah has 128 stickers. Alex has 10 fewer stickers than Sarah. How many stickers does Alex have?

_____ stickers

Chapter 2     forty-one **P41**

## Lesson Check (CC.2.NBT.8)

1. Which number is 10 less than 526?
   - ○ 536
   - ○ 516
   - ○ 426
   - ○ 416

2. Which number is 100 more than 487?
   - ○ 387
   - ○ 477
   - ○ 497
   - ○ 587

## Spiral Review (CC.2.NBT.1, CC.2.NBT.3)

3. Which has the same value as 14 tens? (Lesson 2.2)

   - ○ 1 ten 4 ones
   - ○ 1 ten 9 ones
   - ○ 1 hundred 4 tens
   - ○ 1 hundred 9 tens

4. What is the value of the underlined digit? (Lesson 2.5)

   5<u>8</u>7
   - ○ 8
   - ○ 80
   - ○ 88
   - ○ 800

5. Which number can be written as 30 + 5? (Lesson 1.4)
   - ○ 93
   - ○ 80
   - ○ 53
   - ○ 35

6. Which number can be written as 9 tens and 1 one? (Lesson 1.6)
   - ○ 91
   - ○ 90
   - ○ 19
   - ○ 10

Name _____

## Algebra • Number Patterns

**Lesson 2.10**

COMMON CORE STANDARD CC.2.NBT.8
Use place value understanding and properties of operations to add and subtract.

**Look at the digits to find the next two numbers.**

1. 232, 242, 252, 262, ☐, ☐

   The next two numbers are _____ and _____.

2. 185, 285, 385, 485, ☐, ☐

   The next two numbers are _____ and _____.

3. 428, 528, 628, 728, ☐, ☐

   The next two numbers are _____ and _____.

4. 654, 664, 674, 684, ☐, ☐

   The next two numbers are _____ and _____.

5. 333, 433, 533, 633, ☐, ☐

   The next two numbers are _____ and _____.

**PROBLEM SOLVING**

6. What are the missing numbers in the pattern?

   431, 441, 451, 461, ☐, 481, 491, ☐

   The missing numbers are _____ and _____.

Chapter 2     forty-three **P43**

# Lesson Check (CC.2.NBT.8)

1. What is the next number in this pattern?

   453, 463, 473, 483, ▪
   - ○ 484
   - ○ 493
   - ○ 494
   - ○ 583

2. What is the next number in this pattern?

   295, 395, 495, 595, ▪
   - ○ 395
   - ○ 596
   - ○ 605
   - ○ 695

# Spiral Review (CC.2.NBT.1, CC.2.NBT.3)

3. Which is a way to write the number seven hundred fifty-one? (Lesson 2.6)
   - ○ 751
   - ○ 750
   - ○ 715
   - ○ 705

4. What is the value of the underlined digit? (Lesson 2.5)

   1̲95
   - ○ 1
   - ○ 10
   - ○ 100
   - ○ 1,000

5. Which is another way to write 56? (Lesson 1.5)
   - ○ 506
   - ○ sixty-five
   - ○ 50 + 6
   - ○ 5 tens 5 ones

6. Which of these is a way to show the number 43? (Lesson 1.6)
   - ○ 3 tens 4 ones
   - ○ 4 tens 3 ones
   - ○ 4 tens 13 ones
   - ○ 40 tens 3 ones

Name _____

## Problem Solving • Compare Numbers

**PROBLEM SOLVING
Lesson 2.11**

**COMMON CORE STANDARD** CC.2.NBT.4
Understand place value.

**Model the numbers. Draw quick pictures to show how you solved the problem.**

1. Lauryn has 128 marbles. Kristin has 118 marbles. Who has more marbles?

   _____

2. Nick has 189 trading cards. Kyle has 198 trading cards. Who has fewer cards?

   _____

3. A piano has 36 black keys and 52 white keys. Are there more black keys or white keys on a piano?

   _____

4. There are 253 cookies in a bag. There are 266 cookies in a box. Are there fewer cookies in the bag or in the box?

   _____

Chapter 2

forty-five **P45**

## Lesson Check (CC.2.NBT.4)

1. Gina has 245 stickers. Which of these numbers is less than 245?
   - ○ 285
   - ○ 254
   - ○ 245
   - ○ 239

2. Carl's book has 176 pages. Which of these numbers is greater than 176?
   - ○ 203
   - ○ 174
   - ○ 168
   - ○ 139

## Spiral Review (CC.2.NBT.1, CC.2.NBT.3)

3. Which of these is another way to describe 63? (Lesson 1.4)
   - ○ 60 + 3
   - ○ 6 + 3
   - ○ 30 + 6
   - ○ 30 + 60

4. Which of these is a way to show the number 58? (Lesson 1.6)
   - ○ 80 tens 5 ones
   - ○ 50 tens 8 ones
   - ○ 8 tens 5 ones
   - ○ 5 tens 8 ones

5. Mr. Ford drove 483 miles during his trip. How many hundreds are in this number? (Lesson 2.4)
   - ○ 3
   - ○ 4
   - ○ 8
   - ○ 15

6. Which is another way to write 20? (Lesson 1.5)
   - ○ 202
   - ○ 2 tens 2 ones
   - ○ twenty
   - ○ 2 + 0

Name _____

## Algebra • Compare Numbers

**Lesson 2.12**

COMMON CORE STANDARD CC.2.NBT.4
Understand place value.

**Compare the numbers. Write >, <, or =.**

1. 489
   605

   489 ◯ 605

2. 719
   719

   719 ◯ 719

3. 370
   248

   370 ◯ 248

4. 645
   654

   645 ◯ 654

5. 205
   250

   205 ◯ 250

6. 813
   781

   813 ◯ 781

7. 397
   393

   397 ◯ 393

8. 504
   405

   504 ◯ 405

### PROBLEM SOLVING REAL WORLD

Solve. Write or draw to explain.

9. Toby has 178 pennies.
   Bella has 190 pennies.
   Who has more pennies?

   _____ has more pennies.

Chapter 2

forty-seven **P47**

## Lesson Check (CC.2.NBT.4)

1. Which of the following is true?
   - ○ 123 > 456
   - ○ 135 = 531
   - ○ 315 < 351
   - ○ 331 = 313

2. Which of the following is true?
   - ○ 325 < 254
   - ○ 401 > 399
   - ○ 476 > 611
   - ○ 724 = 742

## Spiral Review (CC.2.OA.3, CC.2.NBT.1, CC.2.NBT.1a, CC.2.NBT.1b, CC.2.NBT.2)

3. Which number has the same value as 50 tens? (Lesson 2.1)
   - ○ 5010
   - ○ 500
   - ○ 50
   - ○ 5

4. Which number has an 8 in the hundreds place? (Lesson 2.5)
   - ○ 44
   - ○ 358
   - ○ 782
   - ○ 816

5. Ned counts by fives. He starts at 80. Which number should he say next? (Lesson 1.8)
   - ○ 805
   - ○ 90
   - ○ 85
   - ○ 75

6. Mr. Dean has an even number of cats and an odd number of dogs. Which of these choices could tell about his pets? (Lesson 1.1)
   - ○ 6 cats and 3 dogs
   - ○ 4 cats and 2 dogs
   - ○ 3 cats and 6 dogs
   - ○ 3 cats and 5 dogs

Name _____

COMMON CORE STANDARDS CC.2.NBT.1,
CC.2.NBT.1a, CC.2.NBT.1b, CC.2.NBT.3,
CC.2.NBT.4, CC.2.NBT.8

# Chapter 2 Extra Practice

## Lesson 2.2 (pp. 61 – 64)

Circle tens to make 1 hundred. Write the number in different ways.

1.

_____ tens

_____ hundred _____ tens

_____

## Lesson 2.3 (pp. 65 – 68)

Write how many hundreds, tens, and ones. Draw a quick picture.

1. 214

| Hundreds | Tens | Ones |
|---|---|---|
|  |  |  |

2. 125

| Hundreds | Tens | Ones |
|---|---|---|
|  |  |  |

## Lesson 2.4 (pp. 69 – 72)

Write how many hundreds, tens, and ones are in the model. Write the number in two ways.

1.

| Hundreds | Tens | Ones |
|---|---|---|
|  |  |  |

_____

_____ + _____ + _____

## Lesson 2.6 (pp. 77 – 80)

Write the number using words.

1. 643

_____

Chapter 2     forty-nine **P49**

## Lesson 2.7 (pp. 81–83)

Read the number and draw a quick picture.
Then write the number in different ways.

1. two hundred sixty-nine

   ____ hundreds ____ tens ____ ones

   _____ + _____ + _____

   _____

## Lesson 2.9 (pp. 89–92)

Write the number.

1. 10 more than 543

   _____

2. 100 less than 256

   _____

## Lesson 2.10 (pp. 93–96)

Look at the digits to find the next two numbers.

1. 577, 587, 597, 607, ▢, ▢

   The next two numbers are _____ and _____.

2. 494, 594, 694, 794, ▢, ▢

   The next two numbers are _____ and _____.

## Lesson 2.12 (pp. 101–104)

Compare the numbers. Write >, <, or =.

1. 312
   321

   312 ◯ 321

2. 233
   219

   233 ◯ 219

# Chapter 3

## School-Home Letter

**Dear Family,**

My class started Chapter 3 this week. In this chapter, we will use different ways to practice our basic addition and subtraction facts.

Love, _____

### Vocabulary

**addend** 4 + 5 = 9
The addends are **4** and **5**.

**sum** 4 + 5 = 9
The sum is **9**.

**difference** 12 − 4 = 8
The difference is **8**.

### Home Activity

Write 5 addition problems (with sums through 10) on individual slips of paper. Write their sums on separate slips. Have your child choose a sum and then match it to the correct addition problem. Repeat until all the problems have been matched correctly with sums.

### Literature

Reading math stories reinforces ideas. Look for these books at the library.

**Cats Add Up**
by Marilyn Burns and Dianne Ochiltree.
Cartwheel Books, 1998.

**Each Orange Had 8 Slices**
by Paul Giganti.
HarperTrophy, 1999.

# Capítulo 3

## Carta para la casa

### Querida familia:

Mi clase comenzó el Capítulo 3 esta semana. En este capítulo, usaremos diferentes modos de practicar nuestras operaciones básicas de suma y resta.

Con cariño, _____

### Vocabulario

**sumando** $4 + 5 = 9$
Los sumandos son **4** y **5**.

**suma** $4 + 5 = 9$
La suma es **9**.

**diferencia** $12 - 4 = 8$
La diferencia es **8**.

### Actividad para la casa

Escriba 5 problemas de suma (con sumas hasta 10) en diferentes pedazos de papel. Escriba los totales en papeles diferentes. Pídale a su hijo que elija un total y lo haga coincidir con el problema correcto. Repita los pasos hasta que todos los problemas concuerden con los totales.

### Literatura

Leer cuentos de matemáticas refuerza los conceptos. Busque estos libros en la biblioteca.

**Cats Add Up**
por Marilyn Burns y Dianne Ochiltree.
Cartwheel Books, 1998.

**Each Orange Had 8 Slices**
por Paul Giganti.
HarperTrophy, 1999.

Name _____

# Use Doubles Facts

## Lesson 3.1

**COMMON CORE STANDARD** CC.2.OA.2
Add and subtract within 20.

Write a doubles fact you can use to find the sum. Write the sum.

1. $2 + 3 = $ ___

   ___ $+$ ___ $=$ ___

2. $7 + 6 = $ ___

   ___ $+$ ___ $=$ ___

3. $3 + 4 = $ ___

   ___ $+$ ___ $=$ ___

4. $8 + 9 = $ ___

   ___ $+$ ___ $=$ ___

5. $6 + 5 = $ ___

   ___ $+$ ___ $=$ ___

6. $4 + 5 = $ ___

   ___ $+$ ___ $=$ ___

# PROBLEM SOLVING  REAL WORLD

Solve. Write or draw to explain.

7. There are 6 ants on a log. Then 7 ants crawl onto the log. How many ants are on the log now?

   _____ ants

Chapter 3 fifty-three **P53**

# Lesson Check (CC.2.OA.2)

1. What is the sum?

    4 + 3 = ___

    ○ 3
    ○ 4
    ○ 6
    ○ 7

2. What is the sum?

    6 + 7 = ___

    ○ 13
    ○ 12
    ○ 7
    ○ 6

# Spiral Review (CC.2.OA.3, CC.2.NBT.1, CC.2.NBT.3, CC.2.NBT.4)

3. There are 451 children in Lia's school. Which of these numbers is greater than 451? (Lesson 2.11)

    ○ 511
    ○ 415
    ○ 399
    ○ 154

4. What number is shown with these blocks? (Lesson 2.8)

    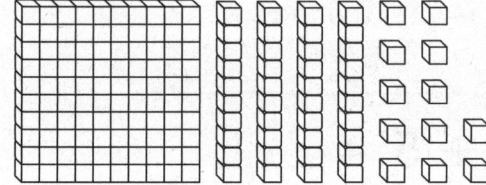

    ○ 112    ○ 152
    ○ 142    ○ 162

5. Which of these numbers has the digit 8 in the tens place? (Lesson 2.5)

    ○ 18
    ○ 278
    ○ 483
    ○ 864

6. Which sum is an even number? (Lesson 1.2)

    ○ 2 + 3 = 5
    ○ 3 + 4 = 7
    ○ 4 + 5 = 9
    ○ 6 + 6 = 12

P54 fifty-four

Name _____

## Practice Addition Facts

**Lesson 3.2**

**COMMON CORE STANDARD** CC.2.OA.2
Add and subtract within 20.

**Write the sums.**

1. 9 + 1 = ___
   1 + 9 = ___

2. 7 + 6 = ___
   6 + 7 = ___

3. 8 + 0 = ___
   5 + 0 = ___

4. ___ = 7 + 9
   ___ = 9 + 7

5. 4 + 4 = ___
   4 + 5 = ___

6. 9 + 9 = ___
   9 + 8 = ___

7. 8 + 8 = ___
   8 + 7 = ___

8. 2 + 2 = ___
   2 + 3 = ___

9. ___ = 6 + 3
   ___ = 3 + 6

10. 6 + 6 = ___
    6 + 7 = ___

11. ___ = 0 + 7
    ___ = 0 + 9

12. 5 + 5 = ___
    5 + 6 = ___

13. 8 + 5 = ___
    5 + 8 = ___

14. 8 + 2 = ___
    2 + 8 = ___

15. 7 + 4 = ___
    4 + 7 = ___

## PROBLEM SOLVING REAL WORLD

Solve. Write or draw to explain.

16. Jason has 7 puzzles. Quincy has the same number of puzzles as Jason. How many puzzles do they have altogether?

    ____ puzzles

Chapter 3

fifty-five **P55**

# Lesson Check (CC.2.OA.2)

1. What is the sum?

    $8 + 7 = \_\_\_$

    ○ 15
    ○ 14
    ○ 12
    ○ 11

2. What is the sum?

    $2 + 9 = \_\_\_$

    ○ 7
    ○ 11
    ○ 12
    ○ 13

# Spiral Review (CC.2.NBT.2, CC.2.NBT.3, CC.2.NBT.4, CC.2.NBT.8)

3. Which is another way to describe 43? (Lesson 1.4)

    ○ 40 + 3
    ○ 30 + 4
    ○ 4 + 3
    ○ 40 + 30

4. Which number is 100 more than 276? (Lesson 2.9)

    ○ 176
    ○ 286
    ○ 376
    ○ 672

5. Which group of numbers shows counting by tens? (Lesson 1.8)

    ○ 10, 11, 12, 13, 14
    ○ 15, 20, 25, 30, 35
    ○ 20, 30, 40, 50, 60
    ○ 60, 59, 58, 57, 56

6. Which of the following is true? (Lesson 2.12)

    ○ 127 > 142
    ○ 142 < 127
    ○ 127 = 142
    ○ 127 < 142

Name _____

# Algebra • Make a Ten to Add

**Lesson 3.3**

COMMON CORE STANDARD CC.2.OA.2
Add and subtract within 20.

**Show how you can make a ten to find the sum.
Write the sum.**

1. $9 + 7 =$ ___

   $1 \quad 6$

   $10 +$ ___ $=$ ___

2. $8 + 5 =$ ___

   $10 +$ ___ $=$ ___

3. $8 + 6 =$ ___

   $10 +$ ___ $=$ ___

4. $3 + 9 =$ ___

   $10 +$ ___ $=$ ___

5. $8 + 7 =$ ___

   $10 +$ ___ $=$ ___

6. $6 + 5 =$ ___

   $10 +$ ___ $=$ ___

7. $7 + 6 =$ ___

   $10 +$ ___ $=$ ___

8. $5 + 9 =$ ___

   $10 +$ ___ $=$ ___

## PROBLEM SOLVING REAL WORLD

Solve. Write or draw to explain.

9. There are 9 children on the bus. Then 8 more children get on the bus. How many children are on the bus now?

   _____ children

Chapter 3

fifty-seven **P57**

# Lesson Check (CC.2.OA.2)

1. Which has the same sum as 8 + 7?
   - ○ 10 + 3
   - ○ 10 + 4
   - ○ 10 + 5
   - ○ 10 + 6

2. Which has the same sum as 7 + 5?
   - ○ 10 + 1
   - ○ 10 + 2
   - ○ 10 + 3
   - ○ 10 + 4

# Spiral Review (CC.2.OA.3, CC.2.NBT.3)

3. Which number can be written as 200 + 10 + 7? (Lesson 2.7)
   - ○ 207
   - ○ 210
   - ○ 217
   - ○ 271

4. Which of these is an odd number? (Lesson 1.1)
   - ○ 2
   - ○ 4
   - ○ 6
   - ○ 7

5. What is the value of the underlined digit? (Lesson 1.3)

   <u>6</u>5
   - ○ 60
   - ○ 50
   - ○ 10
   - ○ 6

6. Which is another way to write the number 47? (Lesson 1.5)
   - ○ 40 + 70
   - ○ seventy-four
   - ○ 4 tens 7 ones
   - ○ 4 + 7

Name _____

## Algebra • Add 3 Addends

**Lesson 3.4**

COMMON CORE STANDARD CC.2.OA.2
Add and subtract within 20.

**Solve two ways. Circle the two addends you add first.**

1. $2 + 3 + 7 =$ _____     $2 + 3 + 7 =$ _____

2. $5 + 3 + 3 =$ _____     $5 + 3 + 3 =$ _____

3. $4 + 5 + 4 =$ _____     $4 + 5 + 4 =$ _____

4. $4 + 4 + 4 =$ _____     $4 + 4 + 4 =$ _____

5.
```
   5        5
   4        4
 + 5      + 5
 ___      ___
```

6.
```
   6        6
   3        3
 + 4      + 4
 ___      ___
```

## PROBLEM SOLVING

Choose a way to solve. Write or draw to explain.

7. Amber has 2 red crayons, 5 blue crayons, and 4 yellow crayons. How many crayons does she have in all?

_____ crayons

Chapter 3 — fifty-nine **P59**

## Lesson Check (CC.2.OA.2)

1. What is the sum of 2 + 4 + 6?
   - ○ 6
   - ○ 8
   - ○ 10
   - ○ 12

2. What is the sum of 5 + 4 + 2?
   - ○ 11
   - ○ 9
   - ○ 7
   - ○ 6

## Spiral Review (CC.2.NBT.1a, CC.2.NBT.1b, CC.2.NBT.3, CC.2.NBT.4, CC.2.NBT.8)

3. Which of the following is true? (Lesson 2.12)
   - ○ 264 < 246
   - ○ 688 > 648
   - ○ 234 = 233
   - ○ 825 < 725

4. Which number can be written as 4 tens 2 ones? (Lesson 1.6)
   - ○ 12
   - ○ 14
   - ○ 24
   - ○ 42

5. Which number has the same value as 50 tens? (Lesson 2.1)
   - ○ 5
   - ○ 50
   - ○ 500
   - ○ 505

6. What is the next number in the pattern? (Lesson 2.10)

   420, 520, 620, 720,
   - ○ 820
   - ○ 850
   - ○ 920
   - ○ 980

Name _____

# Lesson 3.5

## Algebra • Relate Addition and Subtraction

**COMMON CORE STANDARD CC.2.OA.2**
Add and subtract within 20.

Write the sum and the difference for the related facts.

1. 9 + 6 = ____
   15 − 6 = ____

2. 8 + 5 = ____
   13 − 5 = ____

3. 9 + 9 = ____
   18 − 9 = ____

4. 7 + 3 = ____
   10 − 3 = ____

5. 7 + 5 = ____
   12 − 5 = ____

6. 6 + 8 = ____
   14 − 6 = ____

7. 6 + 7 = ____
   13 − 6 = ____

8. 8 + 8 = ____
   16 − 8 = ____

9. 6 + 4 = ____
   10 − 4 = ____

10. 7 + 9 = ____
    16 − 9 = ____

11. 9 + 4 = ____
    13 − 9 = ____

12. 8 + 7 = ____
    15 − 7 = ____

**PROBLEM SOLVING**

Solve. Write or draw to explain.

13. There are 13 children on the bus. Then 5 children get off the bus. How many children are on the bus now?

    ____ children

Chapter 3

sixty-one **P61**

## Lesson Check (CC.2.OA.2)

1. Which is a related addition fact for 15 − 6 = 9?
   - ○ 9 + 6 = 15
   - ○ 3 + 3 = 6
   - ○ 6 + 6 = 12
   - ○ 3 + 6 = 9

2. Which is a related subtraction fact for 5 + 7 = 12?
   - ○ 5 − 2 = 3
   - ○ 15 − 5 = 10
   - ○ 7 − 5 = 2
   - ○ 12 − 7 = 5

## Spiral Review (CC.2.NBT.1, CC.2.NBT.3, CC.2.NBT.8)

3. Which is another way to write 4 hundreds? (Lesson 2.3)
   - ○ 4
   - ○ 40
   - ○ 400
   - ○ 440

4. What is the next number in the pattern? (Lesson 2.10)

   515, 615, 715, 815,
   - ○ 820
   - ○ 905
   - ○ 915
   - ○ 920

5. What number is 10 more than 237? (Lesson 2.9)
   - ○ 227
   - ○ 247
   - ○ 337
   - ○ 347

6. Which is another way to write the number 110? (Lesson 2.7)
   - ○ 100 + 10 + 1
   - ○ 1 hundred 1 ten 1 one
   - ○ one hundred eleven
   - ○ 100 + 10

Name _____

# Practice Subtraction Facts

**Lesson 3.6**

COMMON CORE STANDARD CC.2.OA.2
Add and subtract within 20.

**Write the difference.**

| 1. $15 - 9 = \_\_\_$ | 2. $10 - 2 = \_\_\_$ | 3. $\_\_\_ = 13 - 5$ |
|---|---|---|
| 4. $14 - 7 = \_\_\_$ | 5. $10 - 8 = \_\_\_$ | 6. $12 - 7 = \_\_\_$ |
| 7. $\_\_\_ = 10 - 3$ | 8. $16 - 7 = \_\_\_$ | 9. $8 - 4 = \_\_\_$ |
| 10. $11 - 5 = \_\_\_$ | 11. $13 - 6 = \_\_\_$ | 12. $\_\_\_ = 12 - 9$ |
| 13. $16 - 9 = \_\_\_$ | 14. $\_\_\_ = 11 - 9$ | 15. $12 - 8 = \_\_\_$ |
| 16. $14 - 8 = \_\_\_$ | 17. $10 - 5 = \_\_\_$ | 18. $12 - 5 = \_\_\_$ |
| 19. $15 - 7 = \_\_\_$ | 20. $14 - 9 = \_\_\_$ | 21. $17 - 9 = \_\_\_$ |

## PROBLEM SOLVING  REAL WORLD

Solve. Write or draw to explain.

22. Mr. Li has 16 pencils. He gives 9 pencils to some students. How many pencils does Mr. Li have now?

\_\_\_\_ pencils

Chapter 3     sixty-three **P63**

## Lesson Check (CC.2.OA.2)

1. What is the difference?

    13 − 6 = ____

    ○ 6
    ○ 7
    ○ 8
    ○ 9

2. What is the difference?

    12 − 3 = ____

    ○ 5
    ○ 6
    ○ 7
    ○ 9

## Spiral Review (CC.2.NBT.1, CC.2.NBT.1a, CC.2.NBT.1b, CC.2.NBT.2, CC.2.NBT.3)

3. What is the value of the underlined digit? (Lesson 2.5)

    6<u>2</u>5

    ○ 2
    ○ 10
    ○ 20
    ○ 200

4. Which group of numbers shows counting by fives? (Lesson 1.9)

    ○ 400, 401, 402, 403
    ○ 415, 425, 435, 445
    ○ 405, 410, 415, 420
    ○ 460, 459, 458, 457

5. Devin has 39 toy blocks. What is the value of the digit 9 in this number? (Lesson 1.3)

    ○ 9
    ○ 12
    ○ 30
    ○ 90

6. Which number has the same value as 20 tens? (Lesson 2.1)

    ○ 220
    ○ 200
    ○ 20
    ○ 2

# Use Ten to Subtract

**Lesson 3.7**

**COMMON CORE STANDARD** CC.2.OA.2
Add and subtract within 20.

Name _____

Show the tens fact you used. Write the difference.

1. 14 − 6 = ____

   10 − ____ = ____

2. 12 − 7 = ____

   10 − ____ = ____

3. 13 − 7 = ____

   10 − ____ = ____

4. 15 − 8 = ____

   10 − ____ = ____

5. 11 − 7 = ____

   10 − ____ = ____

6. 14 − 5 = ____

   10 − ____ = ____

## PROBLEM SOLVING  REAL WORLD

Solve. Write or draw to explain.

7. Carl read 15 pages on Monday night and 9 pages on Tuesday night. How many more pages did he read on Monday night than on Tuesday night?

   ____ more pages

Chapter 3 sixty-five **P65**

# Lesson Check (CC.2.OA.2)

1. Which has the same difference as 12 − 6?

   ○ 10 − 6
   ○ 10 − 4
   ○ 10 − 2
   ○ 10 − 0

2. Which has the same difference as 13 − 8?

   ○ 10 − 8
   ○ 10 − 3
   ○ 10 − 5
   ○ 10 − 1

# Spiral Review (CC.2.OA.2, CC.2.NBT.4)

3. Which is a related subtraction fact for 7 + 3 = 10? (Lesson 3.5)

   ○ 10 − 3 = 7
   ○ 10 − 10 = 0
   ○ 7 − 4 = 3
   ○ 7 − 3 = 4

4. Joe has 8 trucks. Carmen has 1 more truck than Joe. How many trucks do they have in all? (Lesson 3.2)

   ○ 7
   ○ 9
   ○ 15
   ○ 17

5. There were 276 people on an airplane. Which of these numbers is greater than 276? (Lesson 2.11)

   ○ 177            ○ 267
   ○ 189            ○ 279

6. Which of the following is true? (Lesson 2.12)

   ○ 537 > 375
   ○ 495 > 504
   ○ 475 < 429
   ○ 201 = 189

P66 sixty-six

Name _____

## Lesson 3.8

# Algebra • Use Drawings to Represent Problems

**COMMON CORE STANDARD CC.2.OA.1**
Represent and solve problems involving addition and subtraction.

**Complete the bar model. Then write a number sentence to solve.**

1. Sara has 4 yellow beads and 3 green beads. How many beads does Sara have?

   | 4 | 3 |

   ____

   _____

   ____ beads

2. Adam had 12 trucks. He gave 4 trucks to Ed. How many trucks does Adam have now?

   | ____ | 4 |
   
   12

   _____

   ____ trucks

3. Grandma has 14 red roses and 7 pink roses. How many more red roses than pink roses does she have?

   | 14 |
   | 7 | |

   ____

   _____

   ____ more red roses

Chapter 3 sixty-seven **P67**

# Lesson Check (CC.2.OA.1)

1. Abby has 16 grapes. Jason has 9 grapes. How many more grapes does Abby have than Jason?

   | 16 |
   |----|
   
   | 9 | ___ |

   - ○ 7
   - ○ 8
   - ○ 15
   - ○ 25

# Spiral Review (CC.2.OA.2, CC.2.NBT.3)

2. Which has the same difference as 16 − 7? (Lesson 3.7)

   - ○ 10 − 10
   - ○ 10 − 6
   - ○ 10 − 7
   - ○ 10 − 1

3. What is the difference? (Lesson 3.6)

   18 − 9 = ___

   - ○ 6
   - ○ 9
   - ○ 10
   - ○ 27

4. Which is another way to write 300 + 20 + 5? (Lesson 2.7)

   - ○ 55
   - ○ 235
   - ○ 325
   - ○ 523

5. What is the value of the underlined digit? (Lesson 1.3)

   <u>2</u>8

   - ○ 80
   - ○ 20
   - ○ 10
   - ○ 2

Name _____

# Algebra • Use Equations to Represent Problems

**Lesson 3.9**

COMMON CORE STANDARD CC.2.OA.1
Represent and solve problems involving addition and subtraction.

Write a number sentence for the problem.
Use a ■ for the missing number. Then solve.

1. There were 15 apples in a bowl. Dan used some apples to make a pie. Now there are 7 apples in the bowl. How many apples did Dan use?

   _____

   _____ apples

2. Amy has 16 gift bags. She fills 8 gift bags with whistles. How many gift bags are not filled with whistles?

   _____

   _____ gift bags

3. There were 5 dogs at the park. Then 9 more dogs joined them. How many dogs are at the park now?

   _____

   _____ dogs

## PROBLEM SOLVING  REAL WORLD

Write or draw to show how you solved the problem.

4. Tony has 7 blue cubes and 6 red cubes. How many cubes does he have in all?

   _____ cubes

Chapter 3    sixty-nine **P69**

## Lesson Check (CC.2.OA.1)

1. Fred peeled 9 carrots. Nancy peeled 6 carrots. How many fewer carrots did Nancy peel than Fred?

   ○ 15
   ○ 6
   ○ 3
   ○ 2

2. Omar has 8 marbles. Joy has 7 marbles. How many marbles do they have in all?

   ○ 1
   ○ 5
   ○ 8
   ○ 15

## Spiral Review (CC.2.OA.2, CC.2.NBT.1)

3. What is the sum? (Lesson 3.1)

   $7 + 8 = ?$

   ○ 2
   ○ 7
   ○ 15
   ○ 17

4. What is the sum? (Lesson 3.4)

   $5 + 4 + 3 =$ _____

   ○ 12
   ○ 15
   ○ 18
   ○ 19

5. Which has the same value as 1 hundred 7 tens? (Lesson 2.2)

   ○ 70 tens
   ○ 17 tens
   ○ 10 tens
   ○ 7 tens

6. Which of the following is a way to describe the number 358? (Lesson 2.4)

   ○ 8 hundreds 5 tens 3 ones
   ○ 5 hundreds 3 tens 8 ones
   ○ 3 hundreds 8 tens 5 ones
   ○ 3 hundreds 5 tens 8 ones

Name _____

# Problem Solving • Equal Groups

**PROBLEM SOLVING**
**Lesson 3.10**

**COMMON CORE STANDARD** CC.2.OA.4
Work with equal groups of objects to gain foundations for multiplication.

**Act out the problem.
Draw to show what you did.**

1. Mr. Anderson has 4 plates of cookies. There are 5 cookies on each plate. How many cookies are there in all?

   _____ cookies

2. Ms. Trane puts some stickers in 3 rows. There are 2 stickers in each row. How many stickers does Ms. Trane have?

   _____ stickers

3. There are 5 books in each box. How many books are in 5 boxes?

   _____ books

Chapter 3

seventy-one **P71**

## Lesson Check (CC.2.OA.4)

1. Jaime puts 3 oranges on each tray. How many oranges are on 5 trays?
   - ○ 8
   - ○ 15
   - ○ 35
   - ○ 53

2. Maurice has 4 rows of toys with 4 toys in each row. How many toys does he have in all?
   - ○ 4
   - ○ 8
   - ○ 16
   - ○ 20

## Spiral Review (CC.2.OA.1, CC.2.OA.2, CC.2.OA.3)

3. Jack has 12 pencils and 7 pens. How many more pencils than pens does he have? (Lesson 3.8)
   - ○ 19
   - ○ 9
   - ○ 6
   - ○ 5

4. Laura has 9 apples. Jon has 6 apples. How many apples do they have in all? (Lesson 3.9)
   - ○ 3
   - ○ 12
   - ○ 15
   - ○ 16

5. Which of these is an even number? (Lesson 1.1)
   - ○ 1
   - ○ 3
   - ○ 5
   - ○ 8

6. What is the sum? (Lesson 3.2)

   $7 + 9 = $ _____
   - ○ 16
   - ○ 17
   - ○ 18
   - ○ 19

Name _____

## Algebra • Repeated Addition

**Lesson 3.11**

**COMMON CORE STANDARD CC.2.OA.4**
Work with equal groups of objects to gain foundations for multiplication.

Find the number of shapes in each row.
Complete the addition sentence to find the total.

1.

   3 rows of ____

   ___ + ___ + ___ = ___

2.

   2 rows of ____

   ___ + ___ = ___

3.

   4 rows of ____

   ___ + ___ + ___ + ___ = ___

4.

   4 rows of ____

   ___ + ___ + ___ + ___ = ___

### PROBLEM SOLVING

Solve. Write or draw to explain.

5. A classroom has 3 rows of desks. There are 5 desks in each row. How many desks are there altogether?

   ____ desks

Chapter 3      seventy-three **P73**

## Lesson Check (CC.2.OA.4)

1. A scrapbook has 4 pages. There are 2 stickers on each page. How many stickers are there in all?

   ○ 4
   ○ 6
   ○ 8
   ○ 10

2. Ben makes 5 rows of coins. He puts 3 coins in each row. How many coins are there in all?

   ○ 9
   ○ 12
   ○ 15
   ○ 18

## Spiral Review (CC.2.OA.2, CC.2.NBT.2, CC.2.NBT.3)

3. There are 5 apples and 4 oranges. How many pieces of fruit are there? (Lesson 3.1)

   ○ 10
   ○ 9
   ○ 8
   ○ 1

4. Which group of numbers shows counting by tens? (Lesson 1.8)

   ○ 35, 40, 45, 50, 55
   ○ 40, 50, 60, 70, 80
   ○ 65, 64, 63, 62, 61
   ○ 70, 71, 72, 73, 74

5. Which is a way to write the number 260? (Lesson 2.6)

   ○ twenty-six
   ○ two hundred six
   ○ two hundred sixteen
   ○ two hundred sixty

6. Which has the same sum as 7 + 5? (Lesson 3.3)

   ○ 10 + 4
   ○ 10 + 3
   ○ 10 + 2
   ○ 10 + 1

Name _____

COMMON CORE STANDARDS CC.2.OA.1, CC.2.OA.2, CC.2.OA.4

# Chapter 3 Extra Practice

**Lessons 3.1 – 3.4** (pp. 121 – 136)
Write the sums.

1. $6 + 6 =$ ___
   $6 + 7 =$ ___

2. ___ $= 7 + 4$
   ___ $= 4 + 7$

3. $0 + 2 =$ ___
   $0 + 8 =$ ___

4. $6 + 9 =$ ___
   $10 +$ ___ $=$ ___

5. $7 + 5 =$ ___
   $10 +$ ___ $=$ ___

6. $4 + 6 + 4 =$ ___

7. $4 + 5 + 3 =$ ___

8. $2 + 7 + 3 =$ ___

9. $2 + 2 + 8 =$ ___

**Lesson 3.6** (pp. 141 – 143)
Write the difference.

1. $9 - 3 =$ ___

2. ___ $= 12 - 5$

3. $16 - 8 =$ ___

4. ___ $= 14 - 6$

5. $11 - 8 =$ ___

6. $12 - 6 =$ ___

7. $5 - 3 =$ ___

8. ___ $= 15 - 9$

9. $7 - 3 =$ ___

10. $12 - 7 =$ ___

11. $14 - 7 =$ ___

12. ___ $= 10 - 7$

# Lesson 3.7 (pp. 145–148)
Show the tens fact you used. Write the difference.

1. 16 − 9 = ___

   10 − ___ = ___

2. 14 − 6 = ___

   10 − ___ = ___

3. 11 − 8 = ___

   10 − ___ = ___

4. 12 − 7 = ___

   10 − ___ = ___

# Lesson 3.9 (pp. 153–156)
Write a number sentence for the problem.
Use a ■ for the missing number.
Then solve.

1. There were 14 birds in the tree. Some birds flew away. Then there were 5 birds in the tree. How many birds flew away?

   _____

   ___ birds

# Lesson 3.11 (pp. 161–164)
Find the number of shapes in each row.
Complete the addition sentence to find the total.

1.

   2 rows of ___

   ___ + ___ = ___

2.

   3 rows of ___

   ___ + ___ + ___ = ___

# Chapter 4

## School-Home Letter

**Dear Family,**

My class started Chapter 4 this week. In this chapter, I will learn how to solve addition problems with 2-digit addends using different strategies.

Love, _____

### Vocabulary

**regroup** To make a group of 10 ones and trade it for a ten

### Home Activity

Pretend you are going on a treasure hunt. Using small pieces of paper, make a path in a small area. Each piece of paper should have an addition problem on it for your child to solve. At the end of the path, place a treasure of some kind.

### Literature

Reading math stories reinforces ideas. Look for these books at the library.

**A Collection for Kate** by Barbara deRubertis. Kane Press, 1999.

**Mission: Addition** by Loreen Leedy. Holiday House, 1997.

# Capítulo 4
# Carta para la casa

## Querida familia:

Mi clase comenzó el Capítulo 4 esta semana. En este capítulo, aprenderé a resolver problemas con sumandos de dos dígitos usando diferentes estrategias.

Con cariño, _____

## Vocabulario

**reagrupar** formar un grupo de 10 unidades y cambiarlo por en una decena

## Actividad para la casa

Jueguen a buscar un tesoro. Con pequeños trozos de papel, haga un camino en un espacio pequeño. Cada trozo de papel deberá tener un problema para que su hijo lo resuelva. Al final del camino, coloque algún tipo de tesoro.

## Literatura

Leer cuentos de matemáticas refuerza los conceptos. Busque estos libros en la biblioteca.

**A Collection for Kate** por Barbara deRubertis. Kane Press, 1999.

**Mission: Addition** por Loreen Leedy. Holiday House, 1997.

Name _____

# Break Apart Ones to Add

**Lesson 4.1**

COMMON CORE STANDARD CC.2.NBT.6
Use place value understanding and properties of operations to add and subtract.

**Break apart ones to make a ten. Then add and write the sum.**

1. 62 + 9 = ____
2. 27 + 7 = ____
3. 28 + 5 = ____
4. 17 + 8 = ____
5. 57 + 6 = ____
6. 23 + 9 = ____
7. 39 + 7 = ____
8. 26 + 5 = ____
9. 13 + 8 = ____
10. 18 + 7 = ____
11. 49 + 8 = ____
12. 27 + 5 = ____
13. 39 + 4 = ____
14. 18 + 8 = ____

## PROBLEM SOLVING  REAL WORLD

Solve. Write or draw to explain.

15. Jimmy had 18 toy airplanes. His mother bought him 7 more toy airplanes. How many toy airplanes does he have now?

____ toy airplanes

Chapter 4

seventy-nine **P79**

# Lesson Check (CC.2.NBT.6)

1. What is the sum?

    26 + 7 = ____

    ○ 96
    ○ 78
    ○ 33
    ○ 19

2. What is the sum?

    15 + 8 = ____

    ○ 7
    ○ 10
    ○ 13
    ○ 23

# Spiral Review (CC.2.OA.1, CC.2.OA.2, CC.2.NBT.3)

3. Hannah has 4 blue beads and 8 red beads. How many beads does Hannah have? (Lesson 3.8)

    ○ 4
    ○ 7
    ○ 10
    ○ 12

4. Rick had 4 stickers. Then he earned 2 more. How many stickers does he have now? (Lesson 3.3)

    ○ 4
    ○ 6
    ○ 7
    ○ 9

5. What is the sum? (Lesson 3.4)

    4 + 5 + 4 =

    ○ 13
    ○ 12
    ○ 11
    ○ 10

6. Which of the following is another way to write 281? (Lesson 2.7)

    ○ 1 hundred 2 tens 8 ones
    ○ 1 hundred 8 tens 2 ones
    ○ 2 hundreds 1 ten 8 ones
    ○ 2 hundreds 8 tens 1 one

P80 eighty

Name _____

**Lesson 4.2**

## Use Compensation

COMMON CORE STANDARD CC.2.NBT.6
Use place value understanding and properties of operations to add and subtract.

**Show how to make one addend the next tens number. Complete the new addition sentence.**

1. 15 + 37 = ?       ___ + ___ = ___

2. 22 + 49 = ?       ___ + ___ = ___

3. 38 + 26 = ?       ___ + ___ = ___

4. 27 + 47 = ?       ___ + ___ = ___

## PROBLEM SOLVING REAL WORLD

Solve. Write or draw to explain.

5. The oak tree at the school was 34 feet tall. Then it grew 18 feet taller. How tall is the oak tree now?

_____ feet tall

Chapter 4

eighty-one **P81**

**Lesson Check** (CC.2.NBT.6)

1. What is the sum?

    18 + 25 = ?

    ○ 43    ○ 31
    ○ 33    ○ 17

2. What is the sum?

    27 + 24 = ?

    ○ 41    ○ 51
    ○ 43    ○ 59

**Spiral Review** (CC.2.OA.2, CC.2.OA.3)

3. Which of the following numbers is an even number? (Lesson 1.1)

    ○ 27
    ○ 14
    ○ 11
    ○ 5

4. Andrew sees 4 fish. Kim sees double that number of fish. How many fish does Kim see? (Lesson 3.1)

    ○ 2
    ○ 8
    ○ 7
    ○ 12

5. Which is a related subtraction fact for 7 + 6 = 13? (Lesson 3.5)

    ○ 13 − 6 = 7
    ○ 7 − 1 = 6
    ○ 7 − 6 = 1
    ○ 13 + 6 = 19

6. What is the sum? (Lesson 3.2)

    2 + 8 = ___

    ○ 0
    ○ 6
    ○ 8
    ○ 10

Name _____

# Break Apart Addends as Tens and Ones

**Lesson 4.3**

**COMMON CORE STANDARD CC.2.NBT.6**
Use place value understanding and properties of operations to add and subtract.

**Break apart the addends to find the sum.**

1.  18  →  ___ + ___
   + 21 →  ___ + ___
           _____
           ___ + ___ = ___

2.  33  →  ___ + ___
   + 49 →  ___ + ___
           _____
           ___ + ___ = ___

3.  72  →  ___ + ___
   + 18 →  ___ + ___
           _____
           ___ + ___ = ___

## PROBLEM SOLVING

Choose a way to solve.
Write or draw to explain.

4. Christopher has 28 baseball cards. Justin has 18 baseball cards. How many baseball cards do they have in all?

_____ baseball cards

Chapter 4

eighty-three **P83**

# Lesson Check (CC.2.NBT.6)

1. What is the sum?

    27
    + 12

    ○ 15
    ○ 19
    ○ 29
    ○ 39

2. What is the sum?

    17
    + 35

    ○ 40
    ○ 42
    ○ 52
    ○ 59

# Spiral Review (CC.2.OA.2, CC.2.NBT.1, CC.2.NBT.3, CC.2.NBT.6)

3. What is the value of the underlined digit? (Lesson 1.3)

    2<u>5</u>

    ○ 5
    ○ 7
    ○ 50
    ○ 55

4. Which has the same value as 12 tens? (Lesson 2.2)

    ○ 10
    ○ 12
    ○ 100
    ○ 120

5. Ally has 7 connecting cubes. Greg has 4 connecting cubes. How many connecting cubes do they have in all? (Lesson 3.2)

    ○ 3      ○ 11
    ○ 8      ○ 25

6. Juan painted a picture of a tree. First he painted 15 leaves. Then he painted 23 more leaves. How many leaves did he paint in all? (Lesson 4.2)

    ○ 8      ○ 33
    ○ 25     ○ 38

Name _____

# Model Regrouping for Addition

**Lesson 4.4**

COMMON CORE STANDARDS CC.2.NBT.6, CC.2.NBT.9
Use place value understanding and properties of operations to add and subtract.

Draw to show the regrouping. Write how many tens and ones in the sum. Write the sum.

1. Add 63 and 9.

   ____ tens ____ ones
   ____

2. Add 25 and 58.

   ____ tens ____ ones
   ____

3. Add 58 and 18.

   ____ tens ____ ones
   ____

4. Add 64 and 26.

   ____ tens ____ ones
   ____

5. Add 17 and 77.

   ____ tens ____ ones
   ____

6. Add 16 and 39.

   ____ tens ____ ones
   ____

## PROBLEM SOLVING  REAL WORLD

Choose a way to solve.
Write or draw to explain.

7. Cathy has 43 leaves in her collection. Jane has 38 leaves. How many leaves do the two children have?

   ____ leaves

Chapter 4     eighty-five **P85**

# Lesson Check (CC.2.NBT.6)

1. Add 27 and 48. What is the sum?

   | Tens | Ones |
   |------|------|

   ○ 27
   ○ 48
   ○ 65
   ○ 75

# Spiral Review (CC.2.OA.2, CC.2.OA.3, CC.2.NBT.6)

2. What is the sum? (Lesson 3.2)

   $7 + 7 =$ ___

   ○ 14
   ○ 13
   ○ 12
   ○ 11

3. Which of these is an odd number? (Lesson 1.1)

   ○ 6
   ○ 12
   ○ 21
   ○ 22

4. What is the sum? (Lesson 4.2)

   $39 + 46 = ?$

   ○ 37
   ○ 58
   ○ 75
   ○ 85

5. What is the sum? (Lesson 3.4)

   $5 + 3 + 4 =$ ___

   ○ 9
   ○ 12
   ○ 14
   ○ 16

Name _____

# Model and Record 2-Digit Addition

**Lesson 4.5**

COMMON CORE STANDARD CC.2.NBT.6
Use place value understanding and properties of operations to add and subtract.

Draw quick pictures to help you solve.
Write the sum.

1.  | Tens | Ones |
    |------|------|
    |      |      |
    |  3   |  8   |
    | +1   |  7   |

    | Tens | Ones |
    |------|------|
    |      |      |

2.  | Tens | Ones |
    |------|------|
    |      |      |
    |  5   |  8   |
    | +2   |  6   |

    | Tens | Ones |
    |------|------|
    |      |      |

3.  | Tens | Ones |
    |------|------|
    |      |      |
    |  4   |  2   |
    | +3   |  7   |

    | Tens | Ones |
    |------|------|
    |      |      |

4.  | Tens | Ones |
    |------|------|
    |      |      |
    |  5   |  3   |
    | +3   |  8   |

    | Tens | Ones |
    |------|------|
    |      |      |

## PROBLEM SOLVING  REAL WORLD

Choose a way to solve.
Write or draw to explain.

5. There were 37 children at the park on Saturday and 25 children at the park on Sunday. How many children were at the park on those two days?

_____ children

Chapter 4

eighty-seven **P87**

# Lesson Check (CC.2.NBT.6)

**1.** What is the sum?

|  | Tens | Ones |
|---|---|---|
|  | 3 | 4 |
| + | 2 | 8 |
|  |  |  |

- ○ 44
- ○ 54
- ○ 52
- ○ 62

**2.** What is the sum?

|  | Tens | Ones |
|---|---|---|
|  | 4 | 3 |
| + | 2 | 7 |
|  |  |  |

- ○ 64
- ○ 70
- ○ 65
- ○ 74

# Spiral Review (CC.2.OA.2)

**3.** Adam collected 14 pennies in the first week and 9 pennies in the second week. How many more pennies did he collect in the first week than in the second week? (Lesson 3.5)

- ○ 25
- ○ 5
- ○ 14
- ○ 3

**4.** What is the sum? (Lesson 3.4)

$3 + 7 + 9 =$ \_\_\_

- ○ 7
- ○ 13
- ○ 10
- ○ 19

**5.** Janet has 5 marbles. She finds double that number of marbles in her art box. How many marbles does Janet have now? (Lesson 3.1)

- ○ 5
- ○ 10
- ○ 15
- ○ 20

**6.** What is the difference? (Lesson 3.6)

$13 - 5 =$ \_\_\_

- ○ 7
- ○ 9
- ○ 8
- ○ 18

# Lesson 4.6

Name _____

## 2-Digit Addition

**COMMON CORE STANDARD CC.2.NBT.5**
Use place value understanding and properties of operations to add and subtract.

**Regroup if you need to. Write the sum.**

1.  4 7
  + 2 5

2.  3 3
  + 1 8

3.  2 8
  + 6 4

4.  1 3
  + 6 5

5.  1 7
  + 2 6

6.  3 6
  + 5 3

7.  5 8
  + 2 5

8.  3 7
  + 4 9

9.  5 2
  + 2 9

10. 6 6
  + 2 4

11. 7 4
  + 1 4

12. 3 7
  + 3 7

### PROBLEM SOLVING  REAL WORLD

Solve. Write or draw to explain.

13. Angela drew 16 flowers on her paper in the morning. She drew 25 more flowers in the afternoon. How many flowers did she draw in all?

    _____ flowers

Chapter 4     eighty-nine     P89

**Lesson Check** (CC.2.NBT.5)

1. What is the sum?

    ```
      2 | 1
    + 3 | 7
    ```

    ○ 16
    ○ 18
    ○ 56
    ○ 58

2. What is the sum?

    ```
      3 | 8
    + 5 | 2
    ```

    ○ 90
    ○ 86
    ○ 80
    ○ 76

**Spiral Review** (CC.2.OA.1, CC.2.NBT.3, CC.2.NBT.8)

3. What is the next number in the counting pattern? (Lesson 2.10)

    103, 203, 303, 403, ___

    ○ 433
    ○ 500
    ○ 503
    ○ 613

4. Rita counted 13 bubbles. Ben counted 5 bubbles. How many fewer bubbles did Ben count than Rita? (Lesson 3.9)

    ○ 8
    ○ 10
    ○ 13
    ○ 18

5. Which number is 100 more than 265? (Lesson 2.9)

    ○ 165
    ○ 275
    ○ 305
    ○ 365

6. Which of the following is another way to write 42? (Lesson 1.5)

    ○ 402
    ○ 40 + 2
    ○ 400 + 2
    ○ 40 tens 2 ones

Name _____

# Practice 2-Digit Addition

**Lesson 4.7**

COMMON CORE STANDARD CC.2.NBT.5
Use place value understanding and properties of operations to add and subtract.

**Write the sum.**

| 1. | 2. | 3. |
|---|---|---|
| 58<br>+ 17 | 44<br>+ 86 | 36<br>+ 13 |
| 4. | 5. | 6. |
| 49<br>+ 72 | 58<br>+ 87 | 32<br>+ 59 |
| 7. | 8. | 9. |
| 77<br>+ 58 | 45<br>+ 45 | 54<br>+ 28 |

**PROBLEM SOLVING**  REAL WORLD

Solve. Write or draw to explain.

10. There are 45 books on the shelf. There are 37 books on the table. How many books in all are on the shelf and the table?

_____ books

Chapter 4

ninety-one **P91**

## Lesson Check (CC.2.NBT.5)

1. What is the sum?

    56
    + 35

    ○ 91
    ○ 81
    ○ 51
    ○ 21

2. What is the sum?

    74
    + 15

    ○ 61
    ○ 69
    ○ 89
    ○ 91

## Spiral Review (CC.2.OA.1, CC.2.OA.2, CC.2.NBT.1, CC.2.NBT.3)

3. What is the value of the underlined digit? (Lesson 2.5)

    5̲26

    ○ 600
    ○ 500
    ○ 50
    ○ 5

4. Mr. Stevens wants to put 17 books on the shelf. He put 8 books on the shelf. How many more books does he need to put on the shelf? (Lesson 3.8)

    ○ 3
    ○ 7
    ○ 9
    ○ 12

5. What is the difference? (Lesson 3.6)

    11 − 6 = ____

    ○ 17
    ○ 15
    ○ 7
    ○ 5

6. Which of these is another way to describe 83? (Lesson 1.4)

    ○ 80 + 3
    ○ 80 + 30
    ○ 30 + 8
    ○ 8 + 3

P92 ninety-two

Name _____

# Rewrite 2-Digit Addition

**Lesson 4.8**

COMMON CORE STANDARD CC.2.NBT.5
Use place value understanding and properties of operations to add and subtract.

**Rewrite the numbers. Then add.**

1. 27 + 19
2. 36 + 23
3. 31 + 29
4. 48 + 23

+ _____   + _____   + _____   + _____

5. 53 + 12
6. 69 + 13
7. 24 + 38
8. 46 + 37

+ _____   + _____   + _____   + _____

## PROBLEM SOLVING REAL WORLD

Use the table. Show how you solved the problem.

9. How many pages in all did Sasha and Kara read?

_____ pages

| Pages Read This Week | |
|---|---|
| Child | Number of Pages |
| Sasha | 62 |
| Kara | 29 |
| Juan | 50 |

Chapter 4

ninety-three **P93**

# Lesson Check (CC.2.NBT.5)

1. What is the sum of 39 + 17?

    +_____

    ○ 66
    ○ 56
    ○ 50
    ○ 22

2. What is the sum of 28 + 16?

    +_____

    ○ 44
    ○ 42
    ○ 34
    ○ 18

# Spiral Review (CC.2.OA.4, CC.2.NBT.1, CC.2.NBT.3, CC.2.NBT.6)

3. Which of the following is another way to write 60 + 4? (Lesson 1.5)

    ○ 46
    ○ 64
    ○ 100
    ○ 604

4. The classroom has 4 desks in each row. There are 5 rows. How many desks are there in the classroom? (Lesson 3.10)

    ○ 9
    ○ 15
    ○ 20
    ○ 35

5. A squirrel collected 17 acorns. Then the squirrel collected 31 acorns. How many acorns did the squirrel collect in all? (Lesson 4.2)

    ○ 14      ○ 21
    ○ 33      ○ 48

6. What number can be written as 3 hundreds 7 tens 5 ones? (Lesson 2.4)

    ○ 753
    ○ 573
    ○ 375
    ○ 357

Name _____

## Problem Solving • Addition

**PROBLEM SOLVING**
**Lesson 4.9**

**COMMON CORE STANDARD** CC.2.OA.1
Represent and solve problems involving addition and subtraction.

Label the bar model. Write a number sentence with a ■ for the missing number. Solve.

1. Jacob counts 37 ants on the sidewalk and 11 ants on the grass. How many ants does Jacob count?

   _____ ants

2. There are 14 bees in the hive and 17 bees in the garden. How many bees are there in all?

   _____ bees

3. There are 28 flowers in Sasha's garden. 16 flowers are yellow and the rest are white. How many white flowers are in Sasha's garden?

   _____ white flowers

Chapter 4

ninety-five **P95**

# Lesson Check (CC.2.OA.1)

1. Sean and Abby have 23 markers altogether. Abby has 14 markers. How many markers does Sean have?

   ○ 9      ○ 7
   ○ 8      ○ 6

2. Mrs. James has 22 students in her class. Mr. Williams has 24 students in his class. How many students are in the two classes?

   ○ 42     ○ 51
   ○ 46     ○ 56

# Spiral Review (CC.2.OA.2, CC.2.NBT.8)

3. What is the difference? (Lesson 3.6)

   $15 - 9 = $ ___

   ○ 24     ○ 14
   ○ 7      ○ 6

4. What is the sum? (Lesson 3.3)

   $7 + 5 = $ ___

   ○ 12     ○ 11
   ○ 10     ○ 9

5. Jan has 14 blocks. She gives 9 blocks to Tim. How many blocks does Jan have now?
   (Lesson 3.5)

   ○ 3
   ○ 5
   ○ 18
   ○ 23

6. What is the next number in the counting pattern? (Lesson 2.10)

   29, 39, 49, 59, ___

   ○ 49
   ○ 69
   ○ 75
   ○ 79

Name _____

## Algebra • Write Equations to Represent Addition

**Lesson 4.10**

**COMMON CORE STANDARD CC.2.OA.1**
Represent and solve problems involving addition and subtraction.

**Write a number sentence for the problem. Use a ■ for the missing number. Then solve.**

1. Emily and her friends went to the park. They saw 15 robins and 9 blue jays. How many birds did they see?

   _____                                   ____ birds

2. Joe has 13 fish in one tank. He has 8 fish in another tank. How many fish does Joe have?

   _____                                   ____ fish

**PROBLEM SOLVING**  **REAL WORLD**

Solve.

3. There are 21 children in Kathleen's class. 12 of the children are girls. How many children in her class are boys?

   ____ boys

Chapter 4                                   ninety-seven **P97**

# Lesson Check (CC.2.OA.1)

1. Clare has 14 blocks. Jasmine has 6 blocks. How many blocks do they have in all?
   - ○ 8
   - ○ 19
   - ○ 20
   - ○ 22

2. Matt finds 16 acorns at the park. Trevor finds 18 acorns. How many acorns do they find?
   - ○ 38
   - ○ 34
   - ○ 32
   - ○ 22

# Spiral Review (CC.2.OA.1, CC.2.OA.2, CC.2.OA.3, CC.2.OA.4)

3. Leanne counted 19 ants. Gregory counted 6 ants. How many more ants did Leanne count than Gregory? (Lesson 3.8)
   - ○ 3
   - ○ 8
   - ○ 13
   - ○ 25

4. What is the sum? (Lesson 3.4)

   $4 + 3 + 6 = $ \_\_\_\_
   - ○ 13
   - ○ 10
   - ○ 9
   - ○ 7

5. Ms. Santos puts seashells into 4 rows. She puts 6 seashells in each row. How many seashells are there altogether? (Lesson 3.11)
   - ○ 12
   - ○ 24
   - ○ 36
   - ○ 42

6. Which of these is an even number? (Lesson 1.1)
   - ○ 9
   - ○ 14
   - ○ 17
   - ○ 21

# Algebra • Find Sums for 3 Addends

**Lesson 4.11**

COMMON CORE STANDARD CC.2.NBT.6
Use place value understanding and properties of operations to add and subtract.

**Add.**

1.
```
  2 3
  2 0
+ 2 5
```

2.
```
  1 5
  2 2
+ 3 8
```

3.
```
  1 3
  5 2
+ 3 4
```

4.
```
  2 7
  4 0
+ 1 9
```

5.
```
  3 1
  4 5
+ 2 4
```

6.
```
  3 4
  1 1
+ 2 8
```

7.
```
  4 2
  3 6
+ 1 1
```

8.
```
  1 8
  2 2
+ 3 4
```

9.
```
  5 3
  1 9
+ 2 5
```

# PROBLEM SOLVING

Solve. Write or draw to explain.

10. Liam has 24 yellow pencils, 15 red pencils, and 9 blue pencils. How many pencils does he have altogether?

_____ pencils

# Lesson Check (CC.2.NBT.6)

1. What is the sum?

   $$\begin{array}{r} 22 \\ 31 \\ +16 \\ \hline \end{array}$$

   ○ 69
   ○ 79
   ○ 83
   ○ 96

2. What is the sum?

   $$\begin{array}{r} 17 \\ 26 \\ +30 \\ \hline \end{array}$$

   ○ 47
   ○ 56
   ○ 63
   ○ 73

# Spiral Review (CC.2.OA.1, CC.2.OA.4, CC.2.NBT.3, CC.2.NBT.8)

3. What number is 10 more than 127? (Lesson 2.9)

   ○ 117
   ○ 137
   ○ 227
   ○ 277

4. Mr. Howard's phone has 4 rows of buttons. There are 3 buttons in each row. How many buttons are on Mr. Howard's phone? (Lesson 3.11)

   ○ 7   ○ 8
   ○ 12  ○ 16

5. Bob tosses 8 horseshoes. Liz tosses 9 horseshoes. How many horseshoes do they toss in all? (Lesson 3.9)

   ○ 15
   ○ 17
   ○ 18
   ○ 27

6. Which of the following is another way to write 315? (Lesson 2.7)

   ○ 1 hundred 3 tens 5 ones
   ○ 3 hundreds 1 ten 5 ones
   ○ 3 hundreds 5 tens 1 one
   ○ 5 hundreds 1 ten 3 ones

Name _____

## Algebra • Find Sums for 4 Addends

**Lesson 4.12**

COMMON CORE STANDARD CC.2.NBT.6
Use place value understanding and properties of operations to add and subtract.

Add.

1.
```
  1 8
  3 2
  2 3
+   3
```

2.
```
  4 5
  3 1
  2 9
+ 7 2
```

3.
```
  2 4
  6 2
  7 0
+ 3 3
```

4.
```
  8 3
  3 2
  6 1
+ 2 2
```

5.
```
  3 7
  1 5
  3 1
+ 1 2
```

6.
```
  2 1
  1 3
  9 6
+ 1 8
```

### PROBLEM SOLVING

Solve. Show how you solved the problem.

7. Kinza jogs 16 minutes on Monday, 13 minutes on Tuesday, 9 minutes on Wednesday, and 20 minutes on Thursday. What is the total number of minutes she jogged?

_____ minutes

## Lesson Check (CC.2.NBT.6)

1. What is the sum?

   $$\begin{array}{r}12\\33\\56\\+32\\\hline\end{array}$$

   ○ 123
   ○ 133
   ○ 131
   ○ 151

2. What is the sum?

   $$\begin{array}{r}41\\74\\43\\+20\\\hline\end{array}$$

   ○ 175
   ○ 188
   ○ 178
   ○ 195

## Spiral Review (CC.2.OA.1, CC.2.NBT.5)

3. Laura had 6 daisies. Then she found 7 more daisies. How many daisies does she have now? (Lesson 3.8)

   ○ 6
   ○ 10
   ○ 13
   ○ 15

4. What is the sum? (Lesson 4.7)

   $$\begin{array}{r}52\\+27\\\hline\end{array}$$

   ○ 89
   ○ 79
   ○ 65
   ○ 16

5. Alan has 25 trading cards. He buys 8 more. How many cards does he have now? (Lesson 4.9)

   ○ 15   ○ 17
   ○ 23   ○ 33

6. Jen saw 13 guinea pigs and 18 gerbils at the pet store. How many pets did she see? (Lesson 4.10)

   ○ 31   ○ 21
   ○ 13   ○ 5

P102 one hundred two

Name _____

COMMON CORE STANDARDS CC.2.OA.1, CC.2.NBT.5, CC.2.NBT.6, CC.2.NBT.9

# Chapter 4 Extra Practice

**Lessons 4.1 – 4.2** (pp. 173 – 180)
Break apart ones to make a ten. Add.

1. 42 + 9 = ____
2. 38 + 7 = ____

Show how to make one addend the next tens number. Complete the new addition sentence.

3. 22 + 49 = ?

____ + ____ = ____

**Lesson 4.3** (pp. 181 – 184)
Break apart the addends to find the sum.

1.  18 ⟶ ____ + ____
   + 26 ⟶ ____ + ____

   ____ + ____ = ____

**Lesson 4.4** (pp. 185 – 188)
Write how many tens and ones in the sum.
Write the sum.

1. Add 45 and 29.

| Tens | Ones |
|---|---|

____ tens ____ ones

____

2. Add 13 and 48.

| Tens | Ones |
|---|---|

____ tens ____ ones

____

3. Add 38 and 18.

| Tens | Ones |
|---|---|

____ tens ____ ones

____

Chapter 4

one hundred three P103

## Lessons 4.5–4.6 (pp. 189–196)

Draw quick pictures to help you solve. Write the sum.

1.  | Tens | Ones |
    |------|------|
    |   4  |   6  |
    | + 3  |   8  |

    | Tens | Ones |
    |------|------|
    |      |      |

2.  | Tens | Ones |
    |------|------|
    |   3  |   2  |
    | + 5  |   7  |

    | Tens | Ones |
    |------|------|
    |      |      |

Regroup if you need to. Write the sum.

3.    5 | 8
     + 1 | 7

4.    4 | 3
     + 2 | 7

5.    3 | 3
     + 5 | 8

## Lesson 4.10 (pp. 209–212)

Write a number sentence for the problem.
Use a ▮ for the missing number. Then solve.

1. Tony has 24 blue marbles and 18 red marbles. How many marbles does he have?

   _____

   _____ marbles

## Lesson 4.11 (pp. 213–216)

Add.

1.     50
       25
    + 19

2.     26
       21
    + 31

3.     64
       17
    + 22

# Chapter 5

## School-Home Letter

**Dear Family,**

My class started Chapter 5 this week. In this chapter, I will learn how to solve 2-digit subtraction problems using different strategies.

Love, _____

### Vocabulary

**minus sign** a symbol used in a subtraction problem

**difference** the answer to a subtraction problem

$$7 - 4 = 3$$
↑
difference

### Home Activity

Write 2-digit numbers, such as 56, 67, and 89, each on a separate index card. Use a pencil and a paper clip to make a pointer for the spinner. Have your child choose a card, spin the pointer, and subtract the number on the spinner from the number on the card.

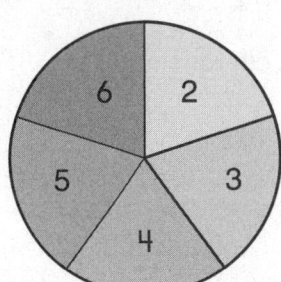

### Literature

Look for these books at the library. Read them with your child to reinforce learning.

**The Action of Subtraction**
by Brian P. Cleary
Millbrook Press, 2006

**The Shark Swimathon**
by Stuart J. Murphy
HarperCollins, 2001

# Capítulo 5

## Carta para la casa

### Querida familia:

Mi clase comenzó el Capítulo 5 esta semana. En este capítulo, aprenderé a resolver problemas de resta de números de 2 dígitos usando estrategias diferentes.

Con cariño, _____

### Vocabulario

**signo de menos** símbolo que se usa en un problema de resta

**diferencia** la respuesta a un problema de resta

$$7 - 4 = 3$$
↑
diferencia

### Actividad para la casa

Escriba números de 2 dígitos, como 56, 67 y 89, cada uno en una tarjeta. Con un lápiz y un clip, haga una flecha giratoria para la rueda. Pida a su hijo que elija una tarjeta, gire la flecha, y reste el número en que se detenga en la rueda del número de la tarjeta.

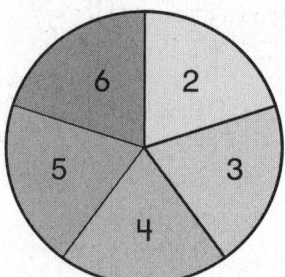

### Literatura

Busque estos libros en la biblioteca. Léalos con su hijo para reforzar el aprendizaje.

**The Action of Subtraction**
por Brian P. Cleary
Millbrook Press, 2006

**The Shark Swimathon**
por Stuart J. Murphy
HarperCollins, 2001

Name _____

## Algebra • Break Apart Ones to Subtract

**Lesson 5.1**

COMMON CORE STANDARD CC.2.NBT.5
Use place value understanding and properties of operations to add and subtract.

Break apart ones to subtract.
Write the difference.

1. 36 − 7 = _____
2. 35 − 8 = _____
3. 37 − 9 = _____
4. 41 − 6 = _____
5. 44 − 5 = _____
6. 33 − 7 = _____
7. 32 − 4 = _____
8. 31 − 6 = _____
9. 46 − 9 = _____
10. 43 − 5 = _____

### PROBLEM SOLVING REAL WORLD

Choose a way to solve. Write or draw to explain.

11. Beth had 44 marbles. She gave 9 marbles to her brother. How many marbles does Beth have now?

_____ marbles

Chapter 5 — one hundred seven **P107**

# Lesson Check (CC.2.NBT.5)

1. What is the difference?

$58 - 9 = \underline{\phantom{00}}$

- ○ 67
- ○ 51
- ○ 49
- ○ 41

# Spiral Review (CC.2.OA.2, CC.2.NBT.6)

2. What is the difference? (Lesson 3.6)

$14 - 6 = \underline{\phantom{00}}$

- ○ 7
- ○ 8
- ○ 9
- ○ 10

3. What is the sum? (Lesson 3.4)

$3 + 6 + 2 = \underline{\phantom{00}}$

- ○ 11
- ○ 10
- ○ 9
- ○ 5

4. What is the sum? (Lesson 4.1)

$64 + 7 = \underline{\phantom{00}}$

- ○ 81
- ○ 73
- ○ 71
- ○ 68

5. What is the sum? (Lesson 4.2)

$56 + 18 = \underline{\phantom{00}}$

- ○ 74
- ○ 72
- ○ 64
- ○ 62

Name _____

## Algebra • Break Apart Numbers to Subtract

**Lesson 5.2**

**COMMON CORE STANDARD** CC.2.NBT.5
Use place value understanding and properties of operations to add and subtract.

Break apart the number you are subtracting. Write the difference.

1. 81 − 14 = _____
2. 84 − 16 = _____
3. 77 − 14 = _____
4. 83 − 19 = _____
5. 81 − 17 = _____
6. 88 − 13 = _____
7. 84 − 19 = _____
8. 86 − 18 = _____
9. 84 − 17 = _____
10. 76 − 15 = _____
11. 86 − 12 = _____
12. 82 − 19 = _____

**PROBLEM SOLVING**

Solve. Write or draw to explain.

13. Mr. Pearce bought 43 plants. He gave 14 plants to his sister. How many plants does Mr. Pearce have now?

_____ plants

Chapter 5 — one hundred nine **P109**

# Lesson Check (CC.2.NBT.5)

1. What is the difference?

$63 - 19 =$ _____

- ○ 82
- ○ 56
- ○ 44
- ○ 36

# Spiral Review (CC.2.OA.1, CC.2.OA.2, CC.2.NBT.6)

2. What is the sum? (Lesson 4.3)

$$\begin{array}{r} 14 \\ + \ 23 \\ \hline \end{array}$$

- ○ 11
- ○ 31
- ○ 37
- ○ 47

3. What is the sum? (Lesson 3.1)

$8 + 7 =$ _____

- ○ 1
- ○ 14
- ○ 15
- ○ 16

4. Which is a related subtraction fact for $6 + 8 = 14$? (Lesson 3.5)

- ○ $18 - 6 = 12$
- ○ $16 - 8 = 8$
- ○ $14 - 8 = 6$
- ○ $8 - 2 = 6$

5. John has 7 kites. Annie has 4 kites. How many kites do they have altogether? (Lesson 3.9)

- ○ 12
- ○ 11
- ○ 7
- ○ 3

P110 one hundred ten

Name _____

# Model Regrouping for Subtraction

**Lesson 5.3**

COMMON CORE STANDARDS CC.2.NBT.9, CC.2.NBT.5
Use place value understanding and properties of operations to add and subtract.

Draw to show the regrouping. Write the difference two ways. Write the tens and ones. Write the number.

1. Subtract 9 from 35.

   _____ tens _____ ones

   _____

2. Subtract 14 from 52.

   _____ tens _____ ones

   _____

3. Subtract 17 from 46.

   _____ tens _____ ones

   _____

4. Subtract 28 from 63.

   _____ tens _____ ones

   _____

## PROBLEM SOLVING REAL WORLD

Choose a way to solve. Write or draw to explain.

5. Mr. Ortega made 51 cookies. He gave 14 cookies away. How many cookies does he have now?

   _____ cookies

Chapter 5     one hundred eleven **P111**

# Lesson Check (CC.2.NBT.9, CC.2.NBT.5)

1. Subtract 9 from 36. What is the difference?

   ○ 45   ○ 26
   ○ 27   ○ 7

2. Subtract 28 from 45. What is the difference?

   ○ 73   ○ 23
   ○ 37   ○ 17

# Spiral Review (CC.2.NBT.5, CC.2.NBT.6)

3. What is the difference? (Lesson 5.1)

   $51 - 8 =$ _____

   ○ 41   ○ 43   ○ 57   ○ 59

4. What is the sum? (Lesson 4.2)

   $38 + 35 =$ _____

   ○ 63
   ○ 67
   ○ 73
   ○ 76

5. What is the sum? (Lesson 4.11)

   $\phantom{+}63$
   $\phantom{+}18$
   $+\phantom{0}9$

   ○ 62   ○ 87
   ○ 80   ○ 90

Name _____

## Model and Record 2-Digit Subtraction

**Lesson 5.4**

COMMON CORE STANDARD CC.2.NBT.5
Use place value understanding and properties of operations to add and subtract.

**Draw a quick picture to solve.
Write the difference.**

1.

| Tens | Ones |
|---|---|
| ☐ | ☐ |
| 4 | 3 |
| − 1 | 7 |

| Tens | Ones |
|---|---|
|  |  |

2.

| Tens | Ones |
|---|---|
| ☐ | ☐ |
| 3 | 8 |
| − 2 | 9 |

| Tens | Ones |
|---|---|
|  |  |

3.

| Tens | Ones |
|---|---|
| ☐ | ☐ |
| 5 | 2 |
| − 3 | 7 |

| Tens | Ones |
|---|---|
|  |  |

4.

| Tens | Ones |
|---|---|
| ☐ | ☐ |
| 3 | 5 |
| − 1 | 9 |

| Tens | Ones |
|---|---|
|  |  |

**PROBLEM SOLVING**  **REAL WORLD**

Solve. Write or draw to explain.

5. Kendall has 63 stickers.
   Her sister has 57 stickers.
   How many more stickers does
   Kendall have than her sister?

   _____ more stickers

Chapter 5  one hundred thirteen **P113**

# Lesson Check (CC.2.NBT.5)

1. What is the difference?

   | Tens | Ones |
   |------|------|
   | ☐    | ☐    |
   | 4    | 7    |
   | − 1  | 8    |

   ○ 55    ○ 29
   ○ 31    ○ 19

2. What is the difference?

   | Tens | Ones |
   |------|------|
   | ☐    | ☐    |
   | 3    | 3    |
   | − 2  | 9    |

   ○ 16    ○ 8
   ○ 12    ○ 4

# Spiral Review (CC.2.OA.2, CC.2.NBT.5, CC.2.NBT.6)

3. What is the difference? (Lesson 3.6)

   10 − 6 = _____

   ○ 5    ○ 3
   ○ 4    ○ 2

4. What is the sum? (Lesson 4.2)

   16 + 49 = _____

   ○ 33    ○ 67
   ○ 65    ○ 75

5. What is the sum? (Lesson 4.1)

   28 + 8 = _____

   ○ 36
   ○ 20
   ○ 18
   ○ 10

6. What is the difference? (Lesson 5.1)

   52 − 6 = _____

   ○ 58
   ○ 50
   ○ 48
   ○ 46

Name _____

# 2-Digit Subtraction

**Lesson 5.5**

**COMMON CORE STANDARD** CC.2.NBT.5
Use place value understanding and properties of operations to add and subtract.

Regroup if you need to.
Write the difference.

1.  | Tens | Ones |
    |------|------|
    |  □   |  □   |
    |  4   |  7   |
    | − 2  |  8   |

2.  | Tens | Ones |
    |------|------|
    |  □   |  □   |
    |  3   |  3   |
    | − 1  |  8   |

3.  | Tens | Ones |
    |------|------|
    |  □   |  □   |
    |  2   |  8   |
    | − 1  |  4   |

4.  | Tens | Ones |
    |------|------|
    |  □   |  □   |
    |  6   |  6   |
    | − 1  |  9   |

5.  |   7  |  7   |
    | − 2  |  6   |

6.  |   5  |  8   |
    | − 3  |  4   |

7.  |   5  |  2   |
    | − 2  |  5   |

8.  |   8  |  7   |
    | − 4  |  9   |

## PROBLEM SOLVING  REAL WORLD

Solve. Write or draw to explain.

9. Mrs. Paul bought 32 erasers. She gave 19 erasers to students. How many erasers does she still have?

_____ erasers

Chapter 5    one hundred fifteen **P115**

# Lesson Check (CC.2.NBT.5)

1. What is the difference?

```
  4 | 8
- 3 | 9
```

   ○ 9     ○ 11
   ○ 10    ○ 19

2. What is the difference?

```
  8 | 4
- 6 | 6
```

   ○ 48    ○ 28
   ○ 38    ○ 18

# Spiral Review (CC.2.OA.1, CC.2.OA.2, CC.2.NBT.5)

3. What is the difference? (Lesson 5.4)

| Tens | Ones |
|------|------|
| ☐    | ☐    |
| 3    | 2    |
| −1   | 9    |

   ○ 11
   ○ 13
   ○ 23
   ○ 51

4. Which of the following has the same sum as 8 + 7? (Lesson 3.3)

   ○ 10 + 2
   ○ 10 + 3
   ○ 10 + 5
   ○ 10 + 6

5. 27 boys and 23 girls go on a field trip to the museum. How many children go to the museum in all? (Lesson 4.9)

   ○ 40    ○ 50
   ○ 44    ○ 54

6. There were 17 berries in the basket. Then 9 berries are eaten. How many berries are there now? (Lesson 3.9)

   ○ 6     ○ 12
   ○ 8     ○ 26

Name _____

# Practice 2-Digit Subtraction

**Lesson 5.6**

COMMON CORE STANDARD CC.2.NBT.5
Use place value understanding and properties of operations to add and subtract.

**Write the difference.**

1.
```
   5 0
 - 1 8
 _____
```

2.
```
   4 3
 - 1 7
 _____
```

3.
```
   7 5
 - 1 8
 _____
```

4.
```
   2 2
 -   6
 _____
```

5.
```
   6 0
 - 3 5
 _____
```

6.
```
   4 2
 - 3 4
 _____
```

7.
```
   2 1
 -   8
 _____
```

8.
```
   3 9
 - 2 7
 _____
```

9.
```
   6 1
 - 3 7
 _____
```

**PROBLEM SOLVING**

Solve. Write or draw to explain.

10. Julie has 42 sheets of paper. She gives 17 sheets to Kari. How many sheets of paper does Julie have now?

_____ sheets of paper

Chapter 5    one hundred seventeen **P117**

## Lesson Check (CC.2.NBT.5)

1. What is the difference?

   $$73 - 47$$

   ○ 24
   ○ 26
   ○ 34
   ○ 36

2. What is the difference?

   $$54 - 13$$

   ○ 31
   ○ 37
   ○ 39
   ○ 41

## Spiral Review (CC.2.OA.2, CC.2.NBT.6)

3. What is the sum? (Lesson 3.2)

   $9 + 9 =$ _____

   ○ 20   ○ 18
   ○ 9    ○ 0

4. What is the difference? (Lesson 3.6)

   $14 - 7 =$ _____

   ○ 21   ○ 13
   ○ 7    ○ 6

5. What is the sum? (Lesson 4.2)

   $36 + 25 =$ _____

   ○ 61
   ○ 54
   ○ 51
   ○ 11

6. What is the sum? (Lesson 3.4)

   $7 + 2 + 3 =$ _____

   ○ 6
   ○ 11
   ○ 12
   ○ 14

Name _____

# Rewrite 2-Digit Subtraction

**Lesson 5.7**

COMMON CORE STANDARD CC.2.NBT.5
Use place value understanding and properties of operations to add and subtract.

Rewrite the subtraction problem.
Then find the difference.

1. 35 − 19

2. 47 − 23

3. 55 − 28

4. 22 − 15

5. 61 − 32

6. 70 − 37

## PROBLEM SOLVING  REAL WORLD

Solve. Write or draw to explain.

7. Jimmy went to the toy store. He saw 23 wooden trains and 41 plastic trains. How many more plastic trains than wooden trains did he see?

_____ more plastic trains

Chapter 5      one hundred nineteen **P119**

# Lesson Check (CC.2.NBT.5)

1. What is the difference for 43 − 17?

   ○ 16     ○ 36
   ○ 26     ○ 60

2. What is the difference for 50 − 16?

   ○ 66     ○ 34
   ○ 46     ○ 24

# Spiral Review (CC.2.OA.2, CC.2.NBT.5, CC.2.NBT.6, CC.2.NBT.9)

3. What is the sum? (Lesson 4.12)

   ```
     29
      4
     25
   + 16
   ```

   ○ 100     ○ 70
   ○ 74      ○ 65

4. What is the sum of 41 + 19? (Lesson 4.7)

   ○ 60
   ○ 50
   ○ 38
   ○ 30

5. Which of the following has the same sum as 5 + 9? (Lesson 3.3)

   ○ 10 + 6
   ○ 10 + 5
   ○ 10 + 4
   ○ 10 + 3

6. What is the difference? (Lesson 5.2)
   45 − 13 = ____

   ○ 28
   ○ 32
   ○ 52
   ○ 58

Name _____

## Add to Find Differences

**Lesson 5.8**

COMMON CORE STANDARD CC.2.NBT.5
Use place value understanding and properties of operations to add and subtract.

**Use the number line. Count up to find the difference.**

1. 36 − 29 = ____

2. 43 − 38 = ____

3. 76 − 68 = ____

## PROBLEM SOLVING  REAL WORLD

Solve. You may wish to use the number line.

4. Jill has 63 index cards. She uses 57 of them for a project. How many index cards does Jill have now?

____ index cards

Chapter 5     one hundred twenty-one **P121**

# Lesson Check (CC.2.NBT.5)

Use the number line. Count up to find the difference.

1. 82 − 75 = ____

   ○ 2     ○ 6
   ○ 5     ○ 7

2. 90 − 82 = ____

   ○ 2     ○ 8
   ○ 4     ○ 9

# Spiral Review (CC.2.OA.1, CC.2.OA.4, CC.2.NBT.5, CC.NBT.9)

3. Jordan has 41 toy cars at home. He brings 24 cars to school. How many cars are at home? (Lesson 5.3)

   ○ 17     ○ 25
   ○ 23     ○ 57

4. Pam has 15 fish. 9 are goldfish and the rest are guppies. How many fish are guppies? (Lesson 3.9)

   ○ 24     ○ 6
   ○ 9      ○ 4

5. What is the sum? (Lesson 4.6)

   ```
     3 | 5
   + 1 | 9
   ```

   ○ 16     ○ 44
   ○ 24     ○ 54

6. Each table has 5 pencils. There are 3 tables. How many pencils are there altogether? (Lesson 3.11)

   ○ 20
   ○ 15
   ○ 8
   ○ 2

Name _____

## Problem Solving • Subtraction

**PROBLEM SOLVING
Lesson 5.9**

**COMMON CORE STANDARD CC.2.OA.1**
Represent and solve problems involving addition and subtraction.

**Label the bar model. Write a number sentence with a ■ for the missing number. Solve.**

1. Megan picked 34 flowers. Some of the flowers are yellow and 18 flowers are pink. How many of the flowers are yellow?

_____ yellow flowers

2. Alex had 45 toy cars. He put 26 toy cars in a box. How many toy cars are not in the box?

_____ toy cars

3. Mr. Kane makes 43 pizzas. 28 of the pizzas are small. The rest are large. How many pizzas are large?

_____ large pizzas

Chapter 5

one hundred twenty-three **P123**

## Lesson Check (CC.2.OA.1)

1. There were 39 pumpkins at the store. Then 17 of the pumpkins were sold. How many pumpkins are still at the store?

   ○ 22   ○ 42
   ○ 26   ○ 56

2. There were 48 ants on a hill. Then 13 of the ants marched away. How many ants are still on the hill?

   ○ 21   ○ 55
   ○ 35   ○ 61

## Spiral Review (CC.2.OA.1, CC.2.OA.2, CC.2.NBT.5, CC.2.NBT.6)

3. Ashley had 26 markers. Her friend gave her 17 more markers. How many markers does Ashley have now? (Lesson 4.10)

   ○ 17   ○ 33
   ○ 26   ○ 43

4. What is the sum? (Lesson 4.7)

   $$\begin{array}{r} 46 \\ + 24 \\ \hline \end{array}$$

   ○ 22   ○ 70
   ○ 60   ○ 72

5. Which of the following has the same difference as 15 − 7?

   (Lesson 3.7)

   ○ 10 − 8
   ○ 10 − 7
   ○ 10 − 3
   ○ 10 − 2

6. What is the sum? (Lesson 4.1)

   34 + 5 = \_\_\_

   ○ 39
   ○ 41
   ○ 49
   ○ 51

Name _____

## Algebra • Write Equations to Represent Subtraction

**Lesson 5.10**

**COMMON CORE STANDARD CC.2.OA.1**
Represent and solve problems involving addition and subtraction.

Write a number sentence for the problem. Use a ■ for the missing number. Then solve.

1. 29 children rode their bikes to school. After some of the children rode home, there were 8 children with bikes still at school. How many children rode their bikes home?

   _____    _____ children

2. 32 children were on the school bus. Then 24 children got off the bus. How many children were still on the bus?

   _____    _____ children

### PROBLEM SOLVING  REAL WORLD

Solve. Write or draw to explain.

3. There were 21 children in the library. After 7 children left the library, how many children were still in the library?

   _____ children

Chapter 5

one hundred twenty-five **P125**

## Lesson Check (CC.2.OA.1)

1. Cindy had 42 beads. She used some beads for a bracelet. She has 14 beads left. How many beads did she use for the bracelet?
   - ○ 22
   - ○ 28
   - ○ 32
   - ○ 56

2. Jake had 36 baseball cards. He gave 17 cards to his sister. How many baseball cards does Jake have now?
   - ○ 19
   - ○ 21
   - ○ 23
   - ○ 41

## Spiral Review (CC.2.OA.2, CC.2.NBT.5)

3. What is the sum? (Lesson 3.2)

   $6 + 7 =$ _____
   - ○ 11
   - ○ 12
   - ○ 13
   - ○ 15

4. What is the difference? (Lesson 3.6)

   $16 - 9 =$ _____
   - ○ 11
   - ○ 9
   - ○ 8
   - ○ 7

5. What is the difference? (Lesson 5.5)

   $$\begin{array}{r} 4\,6 \\ -\,3\,9 \\ \hline \end{array}$$

   - ○ 7     ○ 13
   - ○ 15    ○ 26

6. Which of the following has the same sum as $6 + 8$? (Lesson 3.3)
   - ○ $10 + 2$
   - ○ $10 + 3$
   - ○ $10 + 4$
   - ○ $10 + 5$

Name _____

# Solve Multistep Problems

**Lesson 5.11**

COMMON CORE STANDARD CC.2.OA.1
Represent and solve problems involving addition and subtraction.

**Complete the bar models for the steps you do to solve the problem.**

1. Greg has 60 building blocks. His sister gives him 17 more blocks. He uses 38 blocks to make a tower. How many blocks are not used in the tower?

   _____ blocks

2. Jenna has a train of 26 connecting cubes and a train of 37 connecting cubes. She gives 15 cubes to a friend. How many cubes does Jenna have now?

   _____ cubes

## PROBLEM SOLVING · REAL WORLD

Solve. Write or draw to explain.

3. Ava has 25 books. She gives away 7 books. Then Tom gives her 12 books. How many books does Ava have now?

   _____ books

Chapter 5 one hundred twenty-seven **P127**

# Lesson Check (CC.2.OA.1)

1. Sara has 18 crayons. Max has 19 crayons. How many more crayons do they need to get to have 50 crayons altogether?
   - ○ 13
   - ○ 23
   - ○ 31
   - ○ 37

2. Jon has 12 pennies. Lucy has 17 pennies. How many more pennies do they need to have 75 pennies altogether?
   - ○ 21
   - ○ 35
   - ○ 46
   - ○ 61

# Spiral Review (CC.2.OA.1, CC.2.NBT.5, CC.2.NBT.6)

3. What is the difference? (Lesson 5.2)

   58 − 13 = _____

   - ○ 71
   - ○ 65
   - ○ 45
   - ○ 22

4. What is the sum? (Lesson 4.6)

   ```
     4 | 7
   + 1 | 5
   ```

   - ○ 62
   - ○ 43
   - ○ 52
   - ○ 32

5. There are 26 cards in a box. Bryan takes 12 cards. How many cards are still in the box? (Lesson 5.9)
   - ○ 34
   - ○ 22
   - ○ 18
   - ○ 14

Name _____

COMMON CORE STANDARDS CC.2.OA.1, CC.2.NBT.5, CC.2.NBT.9

# Chapter 5 Extra Practice

## Lessons 5.1 - 5.2 (pp. 229–236)

Break apart the number you are subtracting.
Write the difference.

1. $73 - 7 =$ _____

2. $65 - 7 =$ _____

3. $64 - 8 =$ _____

4. $75 - 18 =$ _____

5. $72 - 12 =$ _____

6. $74 - 19 =$ _____

## Lesson 5.3 (pp. 237–240)

Draw to show the regrouping. Write the difference two ways.
Write the tens and ones. Write the number.

1. Subtract 7 from 52.
2. Subtract 28 from 41.
3. Subtract 16 from 34.

_____ tens _____ ones   _____ tens _____ ones   _____ tens _____ ones

_____   _____   _____

Chapter 5     one hundred twenty-nine   **P129**

# Lesson 5.4 (pp. 241–244)

Draw a quick picture to solve.
Write the difference.

1.  | Tens | Ones |
    |------|------|
    | □    | □    |
    | 4    | 5    |
    | − 1  | 9    |

    | Tens | Ones |
    |------|------|

2.  | Tens | Ones |
    |------|------|
    | □    | □    |
    | 5    | 3    |
    | − 2  | 6    |

    | Tens | Ones |
    |------|------|

# Lessons 5.5 – 5.6 (pp. 245–251)

Write the difference.

1.  7 | 3
   −2 | 8

2.  9 | 5
   −4 | 7

3.  6 0
   −4 8

4.  4 9
   −2 4

# Lesson 5.11 (pp. 269–272)

Complete the bar models for the steps
you do to solve the problem.

1. Ryan buys a pack of 30 stickers.
   His mom gives him 14 stickers.
   How many more stickers does
   he need to have 62 stickers
   in all?

   _____ more stickers

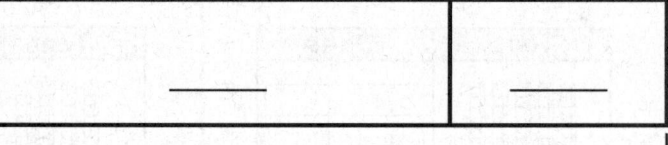

# Chapter 6 School-Home Letter

## Dear Family,

My class started Chapter 6 this week. In this chapter, I will learn how to add and subtract 3-digit numbers, including regrouping ones, tens, and hundreds.

Love, _____

## Vocabulary

**addends** Numbers added together in addition problems

$$7 + 2 = 9$$
↑   ↑
addends

**sum** Answer to an addition problem

$$7 + 2 = 9$$
↑
sum

**difference** Answer to a subtraction problem

## Home Activity

Write addition and subtraction problems with two 3-digit numbers for your child. Write some problems where regrouping is needed and other problems where regrouping is not needed.

$$\begin{array}{r} 462 \\ +341 \end{array} \qquad \begin{array}{r} 796 \\ -578 \end{array}$$

## Literature

Reading math stories reinforces learning. Look for these books at the library.

**A Collection for Kate** by Barbara deRubertis. Kane Press, 1999.

**The Action of Subtraction** by Brian P. Cleary. Millbrook Press, 2006.

Chapter 6     one hundred thirty-one **P131**

# Capítulo 6
# Carta para la casa

## Querida familia:

Mi clase comenzó el Capítulo 6 esta semana. En este capítulo, aprenderé a sumar y restar números de 3 dígitos, incluyendo la reagrupación de unidades, decenas y centenas.

Con cariño, _____

## Vocabulario

**sumandos** números que se suman unos a otros en problemas de suma

$$7 + 2 = 9$$
↑ ↑
sumandos

**suma** resultado de un problema de suma

$$7 + 2 = 9$$
↑
suma

**diferencia** resultado de un problema de resta

## Actividad para la casa

Escríbale a su hijo problemas de suma y resta con dos números de 3 dígitos. Escriba algunos problemas que necesiten reagrupación y otros que no la necesiten.

$$\begin{array}{r} 462 \\ +341 \\ \hline \end{array} \qquad \begin{array}{r} 796 \\ -578 \\ \hline \end{array}$$

## Literatura

Leer cuentos de matemáticas refuerza el aprendizaje. Busque estos libros en la biblioteca.

**A Collection for Kate**
por Barbara Derubertis.
Kane Press, 1999.

**The Action of Subtraction**
por Brian P. Cleary.
Millbrook Press, 2006.

Name _____

# Draw to Represent 3-Digit Addition

**Lesson 6.1**

COMMON CORE STANDARD CC.2.NBT.7
Use place value understanding and properties of operations to add and subtract.

Draw quick pictures. Write how many hundreds, tens, and ones in all. Write the number.

1. Add 142 and 215.

| Hundreds | Tens | Ones |
|----------|------|------|
|          |      |      |

____ hundreds ____ tens ____ ones

_____

2. Add 263 and 206.

| Hundreds | Tens | Ones |
|----------|------|------|
|          |      |      |

____ hundreds ____ tens ____ ones

_____

# PROBLEM SOLVING

Solve. Write or draw to explain.

3. A farmer sold 324 lemons and 255 limes. How many pieces of fruit did the farmer sell altogether?

_____ pieces of fruit

Chapter 6      one hundred thirty-three   **P133**

## Lesson Check (CC.2.NBT.7)

1. Ms. Carol sold 346 child tickets and 253 adult tickets. How many tickets did Ms. Carol sell in all?
   - ○ 113
   - ○ 569
   - ○ 599
   - ○ 699

2. Mr. Harris counted 227 gray pebbles and 341 white pebbles. How many pebbles did Mr. Harris count?
   - ○ 658
   - ○ 568
   - ○ 526
   - ○ 468

## Spiral Review (CC.2.OA.4, CC.2.NBT.5, CC.2.NBT.6)

3. Pat has 3 rows of shells. There are 4 shells in each row. How many shells does Pat have in all? (Lesson 3.11)
   - ○ 7
   - ○ 9
   - ○ 10
   - ○ 12

4. Kara counted 32 red pens, 25 blue pens, 7 black pens, and 24 green pens. How many pens did Kara count in all? (Lesson 4.12)
   - ○ 88
   - ○ 87
   - ○ 81
   - ○ 78

5. Kai had 46 blocks. He gave 39 blocks to his sister. How many blocks does Kai have left? (Lesson 5.8)
   - ○ 8
   - ○ 7
   - ○ 6
   - ○ 3

6. A shop has 55 posters for sale. 34 posters show sports. The rest of the posters show animals. How many posters show animals? (Lesson 5.5)
   - ○ 89
   - ○ 29
   - ○ 21
   - ○ 11

Name _____

# Break Apart 3-Digit Addends

**Lesson 6.2**

**COMMON CORE STANDARD CC.2.NBT.7**
Use place value understanding and properties of operations to add and subtract.

**Break apart the addends to find the sum.**

1.  518 → ____ + ____ + ____
   +221 → ____ + ____ + ____
   
   ____ + ____ + ____ = ____

2.  438 → ____ + ____ + ____
   +142 → ____ + ____ + ____
   
   ____ + ____ + ____ = ____

3.  324 → ____ + ____ + ____
   +239 → ____ + ____ + ____
   
   ____ + ____ + ____ = ____

## PROBLEM SOLVING  REAL WORLD

Solve. Write or draw to explain.

4. There are 126 crayons in a bucket. A teacher puts 144 more crayons in the bucket. How many crayons are in the bucket now?

_____ crayons

Chapter 6                                one hundred thirty-five  **P135**

## Lesson Check (CC.2.NBT.7)

1. What is the sum?

    218
    + 145

    ○ 263
    ○ 363
    ○ 463
    ○ 541

2. What is the sum?

    664
    + 223

    ○ 441
    ○ 881
    ○ 887
    ○ 888

## Spiral Review (CC.2.OA.2, CC.2.NBT.5, CC.2.NBT.6, CC.2.NBT.9)

3. What is the sum? (Lesson 4.2)

    19 + 21 = ?

    ○ 41
    ○ 40
    ○ 39
    ○ 38

4. Which is a related subtraction fact for 9 + 6 = 15? (Lesson 3.5)

    ○ 15 − 9 = 6
    ○ 9 − 6 = 3
    ○ 6 + 9 = 15
    ○ 9 − 3 = 6

5. There are 25 goldfish and 33 betta fish. How many fish are there in all? (Lesson 4.7)

    ○ 8
    ○ 48
    ○ 58
    ○ 68

6. Subtract 16 from 41. What is the difference? (Lesson 5.3)

    ○ 57
    ○ 35
    ○ 25
    ○ 16

P136 one hundred thirty-six

Name _____

# 3-Digit Addition: Regroup Ones

**Lesson 6.3**

COMMON CORE STANDARD CC.2.NBT.7
Use place value understanding and properties of operations to add and subtract.

**Write the sum.**

1.
| Hundreds | Tens | Ones |
|---|---|---|
| | ☐ | |
| 1 | 4 | 8 |
| + 2 | 3 | 4 |

2.
| Hundreds | Tens | Ones |
|---|---|---|
| | ☐ | |
| 3 | 2 | 1 |
| + 3 | 1 | 8 |

3.
| Hundreds | Tens | Ones |
|---|---|---|
| | ☐ | |
| 4 | 1 | 4 |
| + 1 | 7 | 9 |

4.
| Hundreds | Tens | Ones |
|---|---|---|
| | ☐ | |
| 6 | 0 | 2 |
| + 2 | 5 | 8 |

## PROBLEM SOLVING

Solve. Write or draw to explain.

5. In the garden, there are 258 yellow daisies and 135 white daisies. How many daisies are in the garden altogether?

_____ daisies

Chapter 6      one hundred thirty-seven **P137**

# Lesson Check (CC.2.NBT.7)

**1.** What is the sum?

| Hundreds | Tens | Ones |
|---|---|---|
|  | ☐ |  |
| 4 | 3 | 5 |
| + 1 | 4 | 6 |

○ 311   ○ 571
○ 371   ○ 581

**2.** What is the sum?

| Hundreds | Tens | Ones |
|---|---|---|
|  | ☐ |  |
| 4 | 3 | 6 |
| + 3 | 0 | 6 |

○ 712   ○ 742
○ 730   ○ 832

# Spiral Review (CC.2.OA.2, CC.2.NBT.5, CC.2.NBT.6, CC.2.NBT.7)

**3.** What is the difference? (Lesson 3.6)

$9 - 4 =$ _____

○ 13
○ 9
○ 5
○ 3

**4.** What is the sum? (Lesson 4.7)

$$\begin{array}{r} 82 \\ + 59 \\ \hline \end{array}$$

○ 141
○ 64
○ 37
○ 23

**5.** What is the sum? (Lesson 3.6)

$26 + 7 =$ _____

○ 19
○ 32
○ 33
○ 34

**6.** Add 243 and 132. How many hundreds, tens, and ones are there in all? (Lesson 6.1)

○ 3 hundreds 7 tens 5 ones
○ 2 hundreds 7 tens 5 ones
○ 2 hundreds 3 tens 2 ones
○ 1 hundred 1 ten 1 one

# 3-Digit Addition: Regroup Tens

**Lesson 6.4**

COMMON CORE STANDARD CC.2.NBT.7
Use place value understanding and properties of operations to add and subtract.

Write the sum.

1.  | Hundreds | Tens | Ones |
    |---|---|---|
    | ☐ | ☐ |  |
    | 1 | 8 | 7 |
    | +2 | 3 | 2 |

2.  | Hundreds | Tens | Ones |
    |---|---|---|
    | ☐ | ☐ |  |
    | 3 | 2 | 2 |
    | +3 | 5 | 6 |

3.  | Hundreds | Tens | Ones |
    |---|---|---|
    | ☐ | ☐ |  |
    | 2 | 8 | 5 |
    | +5 | 3 | 1 |

4.  4 4 5
   +  3 4

5.  6 2 0
   +2 8 8

6.  5 5 7
   +1 8 0

7.  6 7 1
   +1 5 4

8.  4 6 3
   +4 8 1

9.  7 4 6
   +1 3 3

## PROBLEM SOLVING

Solve. Write or draw to explain.

10. There are 142 blue toy cars and 293 red toy cars at the toy store. How many toy cars are there in all?

_____ toy cars

# Lesson Check (CC.2.NBT.7)

1. What is the sum?

    472
    + 255

    ○ 623
    ○ 627
    ○ 727
    ○ 728

2. What is the sum?

    144
    + 284

    ○ 328
    ○ 418
    ○ 428
    ○ 518

# Spiral Review (CC.2.OA.2, CC.2.NBT.5, CC.2.NBT.7)

3. What is the sum? (Lesson 4.6)

    56
    + 38

    ○ 82
    ○ 84
    ○ 92
    ○ 94

4. What is the sum? (Lesson 6.3)

    326
    + 139

    ○ 465
    ○ 351
    ○ 259
    ○ 187

5. What is the sum? (Lesson 3.1)

    8 + 9 = ____

    ○ 19
    ○ 17
    ○ 9
    ○ 1

6. What is the difference? (Lesson 5.5)

    82
    − 34

    ○ 25      ○ 52
    ○ 48      ○ 56

P140 one hundred forty

Name _____

## Addition: Regroup Ones and Tens

**Lesson 6.5**

**COMMON CORE STANDARD CC.2.NBT.7**
Use place value understanding and properties of operations to add and subtract.

Write the sum.

1.
```
   547
 + 435
 -----
```

2.
```
   367
 + 284
 -----
```

3.
```
   485
 + 456
 -----
```

4.
```
   187
 + 306
 -----
```

5.
```
   647
 + 128
 -----
```

6.
```
   523
 + 174
 -----
```

7.
```
   255
 + 231
 -----
```

8.
```
   294
 + 176
 -----
```

9.
```
   375
 + 364
 -----
```

## PROBLEM SOLVING REAL WORLD

Solve. Write or draw to explain.

10. Saul and Luisa each scored 167 points on a computer game. How many points did they score in all?

_____ points

Chapter 6                        one hundred forty-one  **P141**

# Lesson Check (CC.2.NBT.7)

1. What is the sum?

   348
   + 272

   ○ 136  ○ 520
   ○ 510  ○ 620

2. What is the sum?

   123
   + 217

   ○ 314  ○ 340
   ○ 330  ○ 417

# Spiral Review (CC.2.OA.1, CC.2.OA.2, CC.2.NBT.6, CC.2.NBT.9)

3. Which has the same sum as 9 + 4? (Lesson 3.3)

   ○ 10 + 3
   ○ 10 + 4
   ○ 10 + 5
   ○ 10 + 6

4. What is the sum? (Lesson 4.11)

   32
   15
   + 46

   ○ 47  ○ 83
   ○ 78  ○ 93

5. Add 29 and 35. What is the sum? (Lesson 4.4)

   ○ 16  ○ 64
   ○ 36  ○ 95

6. Tom had 25 pretzels. He gave away 12 pretzels. How many pretzels does Tom have left? (Lesson 5.10)

   ○ 4
   ○ 13
   ○ 37
   ○ 46

P142 one hundred forty-two

Name _____

## Problem Solving • 3-Digit Subtraction

**PROBLEM SOLVING**
**Lesson 6.6**

COMMON CORE STANDARD CC.2.NBT.7
Use place value understanding and properties of operations to add and subtract.

**Make a model to solve. Then draw a quick picture of your model.**

1. On Saturday, 770 people went to the snack shop. On Sunday, 628 people went. How many more people went to the snack shop on Saturday than on Sunday?

    _____ more people

2. There were 395 lemon ice cups at the snack shop. People bought 177 lemon ice cups. How many lemon ice cups are still at the snack shop?

    _____ cups

3. There were 576 bottles of water at the snack shop. People bought 469 bottles of water. How many bottles of water are at the snack shop now?

    _____ bottles

4. There were 279 bags of apple chips at the snack shop. Then 134 bags of apple chips were bought. How many bags of apple chips are at the snack shop now?

    _____ bags

Chapter 6

one hundred forty-three  **P143**

# Lesson Check (CC.2.NBT.7)

1. There are 278 math and science books. 128 of them are math books. How many science books are there?

   ○ 50
   ○ 140
   ○ 150
   ○ 406

2. A book has 176 pages. Mr. Roberts has read 119 pages. How many pages does he have left to read?

   ○ 55
   ○ 57
   ○ 67
   ○ 295

# Spiral Review (CC.2.OA.2, CC.2.NBT.5, CC.2.NBT.6, CC.2.NBT.7)

3. What is the sum? (Lesson 3.4)

   $1 + 6 + 2 =$ _____

   ○ 9
   ○ 8
   ○ 7
   ○ 4

4. What is the difference? (Lesson 5.1)

   $54 - 8 =$ _____

   ○ 62
   ○ 46
   ○ 44
   ○ 34

5. What is the sum? (Lesson 6.5)

   ```
     356
   + 174
   ```

   ○ 182
   ○ 220
   ○ 451
   ○ 530

6. What is the sum? (Lesson 4.3)

   ```
    22
   + 16
   ```

   ○ 47
   ○ 38
   ○ 18
   ○ 6

Name _____

# 3-Digit Subtraction: Regroup Tens

**Lesson 6.7**

COMMON CORE STANDARD CC.2.NBT.7
Use place value understanding and properties of operations to add and subtract.

Solve. Write the difference.

1.

| Hundreds | Tens | Ones |
|---|---|---|
| | ☐ | ☐ |
| 7 | 7 | 4 |
| − 2 | 3 | 6 |

2.

| Hundreds | Tens | Ones |
|---|---|---|
| | ☐ | ☐ |
| 5 | 5 | 1 |
| − 1 | 1 | 3 |

3.

| Hundreds | Tens | Ones |
|---|---|---|
| | ☐ | ☐ |
| 4 | 8 | 9 |
| − 2 | 7 | 3 |

4.

| Hundreds | Tens | Ones |
|---|---|---|
| | ☐ | ☐ |
| 7 | 7 | 2 |
| − 2 | 5 | 4 |

## PROBLEM SOLVING REAL WORLD

Solve. Write or draw to explain.

5. There were 985 pencils. Some pencils were sold. Then there were 559 pencils left. How many pencils were sold?

_____ pencils

Chapter 6                one hundred forty-five  **P145**

## Lesson Check (CC.2.NBT.7)

1. What is the difference?

    346
    − 127

    ○ 119
    ○ 219
    ○ 229
    ○ 473

2. What is the difference?

    568
    − 226

    ○ 342
    ○ 344
    ○ 742
    ○ 794

## Spiral Review (CC.2.OA.1, CC.2.OA.4, CC.2.NBT.5, CC.2.NBT.7)

3. What is the difference? (Lesson 5.1)

    45 − 7 = ___

    ○ 32
    ○ 36
    ○ 38
    ○ 42

4. Leroy has 11 cubes. Jane has 15 cubes. How many cubes do they have altogether? (Lesson 4.10)

    ○ 4
    ○ 15
    ○ 19
    ○ 26

5. Mina puts 5 flowers in each vase. How many flowers will she put in 3 vases? (Lesson 3.10)

    ○ 5
    ○ 10
    ○ 15
    ○ 20

6. Mr. Hill had 428 pencils. He gave away 150 pencils. How many pencils did he keep? (Lesson 6.6)

    ○ 278
    ○ 338
    ○ 350
    ○ 578

P146  one hundred forty-six

Name _____

# 3-Digit Subtraction: Regroup Hundreds

**Lesson 6.8**

**COMMON CORE STANDARD CC.2.NBT.7**
Use place value understanding and properties of operations to add and subtract.

**Solve. Write the difference.**

1.

| Hundreds | Tens | Ones |
|---|---|---|
| ☐ | ☐ | ☐ |
| 7 | 2 | 7 |
| − 2 | 5 | 6 |

2.

| Hundreds | Tens | Ones |
|---|---|---|
| ☐ | ☐ | ☐ |
| 9 | 6 | 7 |
| − 1 | 5 | 3 |

3.

| | | |
|---|---|---|
| 6 | 3 | 9 |
| − 4 | 7 | 2 |

4.

| | | |
|---|---|---|
| 4 | 4 | 8 |
| − 3 | 6 | 3 |

## PROBLEM SOLVING  REAL WORLD

Solve. Write or draw to explain.

5. There were 537 people in the parade. 254 of these people were playing an instrument. How many people were not playing an instrument?

_____ people

Chapter 6

one hundred forty-seven **P147**

# Lesson Check (CC.2.NBT.7)

1. What is the difference?

    538
    − 135

    ○ 403
    ○ 463
    ○ 663
    ○ 673

2. What is the difference?

    218
    − 126

    ○ 82
    ○ 92
    ○ 132
    ○ 192

# Spiral Review (CC.2.OA.2, CC.2.NBT.5, CC.2.NBT.6, CC.2.NBT.7)

3. What is the difference? (Lesson 5.2)

    52 − 15 = _____

    ○ 63
    ○ 43
    ○ 37
    ○ 33

4. What is the sum? (Lesson 3.2)

    8 + 7 = _____

    ○ 1
    ○ 9
    ○ 14
    ○ 15

5. What is the sum? (Lesson 4.5)

    47
    + 26

    ○ 73
    ○ 65
    ○ 46
    ○ 21

6. What is the difference? (Lesson 6.7)

    392
    − 173

    ○ 565
    ○ 361
    ○ 246
    ○ 219

P148  one hundred forty-eight

Name _____

# Subtraction: Regroup Hundreds and Tens

**Lesson 6.9**

COMMON CORE STANDARD CC.2.NBT.7
Use place value understanding and properties of operations to add and subtract.

**Solve. Write the difference.**

1.
```
  8 1 6
- 3 4 5
```

2.
```
  9 4 2
- 1 6 3
```

3.
```
  7 9 6
- 4 6 8
```

4.
```
  7 2 3
- 5 4 3
```

5.
```
  9 8 6
- 7 1 2
```

6.
```
  5 4 7
- 2 8 9
```

**PROBLEM SOLVING**  REAL WORLD

Solve.

7. Mia's coloring book has 432 pages. She has already colored 178 pages. How many pages in the book are left to color?

_____ pages

Chapter 6      one hundred forty-nine   **P149**

# Lesson Check (CC.2.NBT.7)

1. What is the difference?

    349
    − 187
    _____

    ○ 162
    ○ 242
    ○ 462
    ○ 536

2. What is the difference?

    336
    − 178
    _____

    ○ 242
    ○ 188
    ○ 168
    ○ 158

# Spiral Review (CC.2.OA.1, CC.2.OA.2, CC.2.NBT.5, CC.2.NBT.7)

3. What is the sum? (Lesson 6.2)

    246
    + 533
    _____

    ○ 313
    ○ 719
    ○ 773
    ○ 779

4. What is the difference? (Lesson 5.6)

    38
    − 14
    _____

    ○ 52
    ○ 24
    ○ 18
    ○ 12

5. What is the difference? (Lesson 3.7)

    17 − 9 = ____

    ○ 8
    ○ 9
    ○ 10
    ○ 12

6. Lisa had 15 daisies. She gave away 7 daisies. Then she found 3 more daisies. How many daisies does Lisa have now? (Lesson 5.11)

    ○ 25
    ○ 19
    ○ 13
    ○ 11

P150 one hundred fifty

Name _____

# Regrouping with Zeros

**Lesson 6.10**

**COMMON CORE STANDARD** CC.2.NBT.7
Use place value understanding and properties of operations to add and subtract.

**Solve. Write the difference.**

1.
```
  8 0 6
- 3 4 5
```

2.
```
  9 0 2
- 7 8 3
```

3.
```
  7 9 4
- 2 6 8
```

4.
```
  6 8 7
- 1 4 4
```

5.
```
  5 0 5
- 1 6 7
```

6.
```
  3 0 7
- 1 5 4
```

## PROBLEM SOLVING — REAL WORLD

Solve.

7. There are 303 students.
There are 147 girls.
How many boys are there?

_____ boys

## Lesson Check (CC.2.NBT.7)

1. What is the difference?

   $$\begin{array}{r}301\\-187\\\hline\end{array}$$

   - ○ 114
   - ○ 116
   - ○ 186
   - ○ 286

2. What is the difference?

   $$\begin{array}{r}406\\-268\\\hline\end{array}$$

   - ○ 128
   - ○ 138
   - ○ 162
   - ○ 262

## Spiral Review (CC.2.OA.2, CC.2.NBT.5, CC.2.NBT.7, CC.2.NBT.9)

3. What is the sum? (Lesson 4.7)

   $$\begin{array}{r}35\\+79\\\hline\end{array}$$

   - ○ 44
   - ○ 62
   - ○ 104
   - ○ 114

4. What is the sum? (Lesson 6.4)

   $$\begin{array}{r}555\\+282\\\hline\end{array}$$

   - ○ 847
   - ○ 837
   - ○ 737
   - ○ 273

5. What is the difference? (Lesson 3.6)

   $10 - 2 = $ ___

   - ○ 12
   - ○ 9
   - ○ 8
   - ○ 7

6. Subtract 11 from 43. What is the difference? (Lesson 5.3)

   - ○ 32
   - ○ 34
   - ○ 42
   - ○ 52

Name _____

COMMON CORE STANDARD CC.2.NBT.7

# Chapter 6 Extra Practice

## Lesson 6.2 (pp. 285–288)
Break apart the addends to find the sum.

1.   121 ⟶  ____ + ____ + ____

    + 269 ⟶  ____ + ____ + ____

              ____ + ____ + ____ = ____

## Lesson 6.3 (pp. 289–292)
Write the sum.

1.
| Hundreds | Tens | Ones |
|---|---|---|
|  | ☐ |  |
| 6 | 5 | 8 |
| + 2 | 1 | 6 |

2.
| Hundreds | Tens | Ones |
|---|---|---|
|  | ☐ |  |
| 4 | 0 | 3 |
| + 3 | 2 | 9 |

## Lessons 6.4 – 6.5 (pp. 293–299)
Write the sum.

1.  
| 2 | 9 | 3 |
|---|---|---|
| + 5 | 8 | 5 |

2.  
  3 6 8
+ 4 6 4

3.  
  1 7 6
+ 3 4 8

Chapter 6     one hundred fifty-three **P153**

# Lesson 6.6 (pp. 301–304)
Make a model to solve. Then draw a quick picture of your model.

1. There are 485 books on the shelves and 114 books on the tables. How many more books are on the shelves than on the tables?

_____ more books

# Lesson 6.7 (pp. 305–308)
Solve. Write the difference.

1.  

| Hundreds | Tens | Ones |
|---|---|---|
| 6 | 8 | 1 |
| − 3 | 1 | 2 |

2.  

| Hundreds | Tens | Ones |
|---|---|---|
| 7 | 3 | 4 |
| − 5 | 2 | 6 |

# Lesson 6.8 (pp. 309–312)
Solve. Write the difference.

1.  

| 6 | 1 | 3 |
|---|---|---|
| − 2 | 8 | 3 |

2.  

| 8 | 7 | 5 |
|---|---|---|
| − 2 | 8 | 3 |

P154 one hundred fifty-four

# Chapter 7

## School-Home Letter

**Dear Family,**

My class started Chapter 7 this week. In this chapter, I will learn about the values of coins and how to find the total value of a group of money. I will also learn how to tell time on analog clocks and digital clocks.

Love, _____

### Vocabulary

**penny** a coin with a value of 1 cent

**nickel** a coin with a value of 5 cents

**dime** a coin with a value of 10 cents

**quarter** a coin with a value of 25 cents

**dollar** an amount equal to 100 cents

**minute** a unit of time

### Home Activity

With your child, set up a play store together. Use objects such as food items or small toys. Put price tags on each object, using amounts less than one dollar. On a sheet of paper, have your child write the price of an object and then draw a group of coins that has that as its total value. Take turns doing this for several objects.

### Literature

Reading math stories reinforces ideas. Look for these books at the library.

*A Dollar for Penny* by Julie Glass Random House Books for Young Readers, 2000

*What Time Is It, Mr. Crocodile?* by Judy Sierra Gulliver Books, 2004

# Capítulo 7

# Carta para la casa

## Querida familia:

Mi clase comenzó el Capítulo 7 esta semana. En este capítulo, aprenderé sobre el valor de las monedas y cómo hallar el valor total de una cantidad de dinero. También aprenderé a decir la hora usando relojes analógicos y relojes digitales.

Con cariño, _____

## Vocabulario

**moneda de 1¢** una moneda con un valor de 1 centavo

**moneda de 5¢** una moneda con un valor de 5 centavos

**moneda de 10¢** una moneda con valor de 10 centavos

**moneda de 25¢** una moneda con un valor de 25 centavos

**dólar** una cantidad igual a 100 centavos

**minuto** una unidad de tiempo

## Actividad para la casa

Junto a su hijo, jueguen a que están en una tienda. Use objetos tales como artículos de comida o juguetes pequeños. Coloque etiquetas en cada artículo con un precio menor a un dólar. En una hoja de papel, pida su hijo que escriba el precio de un objeto y que dibuje un grupo de monedas que muestren ese valor. Túrnense para repetir la actividad con diferentes objetos.

## Literatura

Leer cuentos de matemáticas refuerza los conceptos. Busque estos libros en la biblioteca.

**A Dollar for Penny**
por Julie Glass.
Random House Books for Young Readers, 2000.

**What Time Is It, Mr. Crocodile?**
por Judy Sierra.
Gulliver Books, 2004.

Name _____

# Dimes, Nickels, and Pennies

**Lesson 7.1**

COMMON CORE STANDARD CC.2.MD.8
Work with time and money.

Count on to find the total value.

1.

   ☐ total value

2.

   ☐ total value

3.

   ☐ total value

4.

   ☐ total value

# PROBLEM SOLVING REAL WORLD

Solve. Write or draw to explain.

5. Aaron has 5 dimes and 2 nickels. How much money does Aaron have?

Chapter 7     one hundred fifty-seven **P157**

# Lesson Check (CC.2.MD.8)

1. What is the total value of this group of coins?

- ○ 21¢
- ○ 26¢
- ○ 31¢
- ○ 36¢

# Spiral Review (CC.2.OA.2, CC.2.OA.4, CC.2.NBT.1, CC.2.NBT.2)

2. Hayden is building toy cars. Each car needs 4 wheels. How many wheels will Hayden use to build 3 toy cars? (Lesson 3.10)
   - ○ 7
   - ○ 8
   - ○ 12
   - ○ 16

3. What is the value of the underlined digit? (Lesson 2.5)

   <u>4</u>29
   - ○ 4
   - ○ 40
   - ○ 44
   - ○ 400

4. Which group of numbers shows counting by fives? (Lesson 1.8)
   - ○ 76, 75, 74, 73, 72
   - ○ 55, 56, 57, 58, 59
   - ○ 40, 45, 50, 55, 60
   - ○ 10, 20, 30, 40, 50

5. What is the difference? (Lesson 3.7)

   12 − 7 = _____
   - ○ 5
   - ○ 9
   - ○ 10
   - ○ 19

P158 one hundred fifty-eight

Name _____

# Quarters

**Lesson 7.2**

COMMON CORE STANDARD CC.2.MD.8
Work with time and money.

Count on to find the total value.

1.

   _____  □ total value

2.

   _____  □ total value

3.

   _____  □ total value

**PROBLEM SOLVING**  REAL WORLD

Read the clue. Choose the name of a coin from the box to answer the question.

| nickel | dime |
| quarter | penny |

4. I have the same value as a group of 2 dimes and 1 nickel. What coin am I?

   _____

Chapter 7

## Lesson Check (CC.2.MD.8)

1. What is the total value of this group of coins?

○ 61¢    ○ 63¢    ○ 65¢    ○ 70¢

## Spiral Review (CC.2.OA.1, CC.2.OA.3, CC.2NBT.3, CC.2NBT.4)

2. Which of these is an odd number? (Lesson 1.1)

   ○ 8
   ○ 14
   ○ 17
   ○ 22

3. Kai scored 4 points and Gail scored 7 points. How many points did they score altogether? (Lesson 3.9)

   ○ 15
   ○ 11
   ○ 10
   ○ 3

4. There were 382 chairs in the music hall. Which number is greater than 382? (Lesson 2.11)

   ○ 423
   ○ 328
   ○ 283
   ○ 182

5. Which is another way to write the number 61? (Lesson 1.5)

   ○ 16
   ○ sixty-one
   ○ 60 + 10
   ○ 6 tens 6 ones

P160 one hundred sixty

Name _____

## Count Collections

**Lesson 7.3**

COMMON CORE STANDARD CC.2.MD.8
Work with time and money.

Draw and label the coins from greatest to least value. Find the total value.

1.

_____

2.

_____

3.

_____

## PROBLEM SOLVING  REAL WORLD

Solve. Write or draw to explain.

4. Rebecca has these coins. She spends 1 quarter. How much money does she have left?

_____

Chapter 7 · one hundred sixty-one P161

## Lesson Check (CC.2.MD.8)

1. What is the total value of this group of coins?

○ 22¢      ○ 47¢      ○ 51¢      ○ 65¢

## Spiral Review (CC.2.OA.2, CC.2.NBT.1, CC.2.NBT.3, CC.2.NBT.8)

2. Which number is 100 more than 562? (Lesson 2.9)

   ○ 662
   ○ 572
   ○ 552
   ○ 462

3. Which of these is another way to describe 58? (Lesson 1.4)

   ○ 8 + 5
   ○ 50 + 8
   ○ 80 + 5
   ○ 50 + 80

4. What is the sum? (Lesson 3.2)

   6 + 3 = _____

   ○ 3
   ○ 6
   ○ 9
   ○ 18

5. What number do the blocks show? (Lesson 2.4)

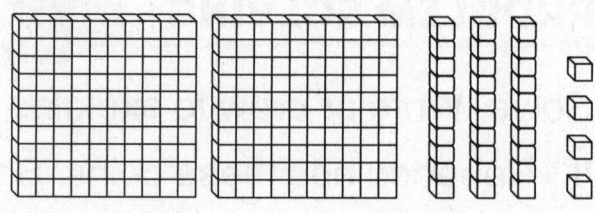

   ○ 134      ○ 243
   ○ 234      ○ 423

P162 one hundred sixty-two

Name _____

# Show Amounts in Two Ways

**HANDS ON
Lesson 7.4**

**COMMON CORE STANDARD** CC.2.MD.8
Work with time and money.

Use coins. Show the amounts in two ways.
Draw and label the coins.

1. 39¢

2. 70¢

3. 57¢

# PROBLEM SOLVING

4. Madeline uses fewer than 5 coins to pay 60¢. Draw coins to show one way she could pay 60¢.

**Chapter 7**

one hundred sixty-three **P163**

# Lesson Check (CC.2.MD.8)

1. Which group of coins has the same total value?

# Spiral Review (CC.2.OA.2, CC.2NBT.1, CC.2NBT.3)

2. Which of these is another way to show the number 31? (Lesson 1.6)

   ○ 1 ten 3 ones
   ○ 1 ten 13 ones
   ○ 2 tens 3 ones
   ○ 2 tens 11 ones

3. Which has the same value as 13 tens? (Lesson 2.2)

   ○ 1 hundred 3 tens
   ○ 3 hundreds 3 tens
   ○ 3 tens 1 one
   ○ 1 ten 3 ones

4. What is the value of the underlined digit? (Lesson 1.3)

   2<u>8</u>

   ○ 2
   ○ 8
   ○ 18
   ○ 80

5. What is the sum? (Lesson 3.1)

   5 + 6 = \_\_\_\_

   ○ 1
   ○ 10
   ○ 11
   ○ 13

Name _____

# One Dollar

**Lesson 7.5**

**COMMON CORE STANDARD** CC.2.MD.8
Work with time and money.

Circle coins to make $1.00.
Cross out the coins you do not use.

1.

2.

3.

## PROBLEM SOLVING

4. Draw more coins to show $1.00 in all.

Chapter 7      one hundred sixty-five **P165**

# Lesson Check (CC.2.MD.8)

1. Which group of coins has a value of $1.00?

○ ○ ○

# Spiral Review (CC.2.OA.3, CC.2.NBT.2, CC.2.NBT.3, CC.2.MD.8)

2. Which is another way to write 692? (Lesson 2.7)

   ○ six hundred ninety-two
   ○ 600 + 9 + 2
   ○ six hundred nineteen
   ○ 60 + 90 + 2

3. Which sum is an even number? (Lesson 1.2)

   ○ 5 + 4 = 9
   ○ 6 + 5 = 11
   ○ 7 + 7 = 14
   ○ 8 + 9 = 17

4. Which group of coins has a total value of 40¢? (Lesson 7.4)

   ○ 4 quarters
   ○ 4 dimes and 1 nickel
   ○ 1 quarter and 3 nickels
   ○ 2 dimes and 2 pennies

5. Which group of numbers shows counting by tens? (Lesson 1.9)

   ○ 110, 109, 108, 107
   ○ 115, 116, 117, 118
   ○ 220, 225, 230, 235
   ○ 230, 240, 250, 260

Name _____

# Amounts Greater Than $1

**Lesson 7.6**

COMMON CORE STANDARD CC.2.MD.8
Work with time and money.

Circle the money that makes $1.00. Then write the total value of the money shown.

1.

   _____

2.

   _____

3.

   _____

## PROBLEM SOLVING  REAL WORLD

Solve. Write or draw to explain.

4. Grace found 3 quarters, 3 dimes, and 1 nickel in her pocket. How much money did she find?

   _____

Chapter 7      one hundred sixty-seven **P167**

# Lesson Check (CC.2.MD.8)

1. Julie has this money in her bank. What is the total value of this money?

- ○ $1.10
- ○ $1.25
- ○ $1.30
- ○ $1.35

# Spiral Review (CC.2.OA.2, CC.2.NBT.5, CC.2.NBT.8)

2. What is the sum? (Lesson 4.7)

```
  7 9
+ 4 2
```

- ○ 37
- ○ 111
- ○ 121
- ○ 127

3. What is the difference? (Lesson 5.5)

```
  6 1
- 2 7
```

- ○ 28
- ○ 34
- ○ 48
- ○ 88

4. Which number is 100 less than 694? (Lesson 2.9)

- ○ 594
- ○ 684
- ○ 704
- ○ 794

5. Which of the following has the same sum as 6 + 5? (Lesson 3.3)

- ○ 10 + 6
- ○ 10 + 5
- ○ 10 + 3
- ○ 10 + 1

Name _____

## Problem Solving • Money

**PROBLEM SOLVING**
**Lesson 7.7**

**COMMON CORE STANDARD** CC.2.MD.8
Work with time and money.

**Use play coins and bills to solve.
Draw to show what you did.**

1. Sara has 2 quarters, 1 nickel, and two $1 bills. How much money does Sara have? _____

2. Brad has one $1 bill, 4 dimes, and 2 nickels in his bank. How much money does Brad have in his bank? _____

3. Mr. Morgan gives 1 quarter, 3 nickels, 4 pennies, and one $1 bill to the clerk. How much money does Mr. Morgan give the clerk? _____

Chapter 7

one hundred sixty-nine **P169**

## Lesson Check (CC.2.MD.8)

1. Lee has two $1 bills and 4 dimes. How much money does Lee have?
   - ○ $1.40
   - ○ $2.40
   - ○ $2.50
   - ○ $2.90

2. Dawn has 2 quarters, 1 nickel, and one $1 bill. How much money does Dawn have?
   - ○ $1.05
   - ○ $1.25
   - ○ $1.55
   - ○ $2.55

## Spiral Review (CC.2.OA.2, CC.2.NBT.3, CC.2.NBT.4, CC.2.NBT.8)

3. What is the value of the underlined digit? (Lesson 1.3)

   5<u>6</u>
   - ○ 5
   - ○ 6
   - ○ 16
   - ○ 60

4. Which of the following is true? (Lesson 2.12)
   - ○ 342 > 243
   - ○ 142 > 162
   - ○ 280 > 306
   - ○ 417 < 380

5. What is the difference? (Lesson 3.6)

   15 − 8 = _____
   - ○ 7
   - ○ 9
   - ○ 15
   - ○ 23

6. What is the next number in this pattern? (Lesson 2.10)

   225, 325, 425, 525,
   - ○ 445
   - ○ 535
   - ○ 625
   - ○ 645

**P170** one hundred seventy

Name _____

# Time to the Hour and Half Hour

**Lesson 7.8**

COMMON CORE STANDARD CC.2.MD.7
Work with time and money.

Look at the clock hands. Write the time.

1.

2.

3.

4.

5.

6.

## PROBLEM SOLVING

7. Amy's music lesson begins at 4:00. Draw hands on the clock to show this time.

Chapter 7

one hundred seventy-one **P171**

## Lesson Check (CC.2.MD.7)

1. What is the time on this clock?

   ○ 3:00
   ○ 3:30
   ○ 4:00
   ○ 4:30

2. What is the time on this clock?

   ○ 12:00
   ○ 12:30
   ○ 6:00
   ○ 6:30

## Spiral Review (CC.2.OA.3, CC.2.NBT.1, CC.2.NBT.4, CC.2.MD.8)

3. Rachel has one $1 bill, 3 quarters, and 2 pennies. How much money does Rachel have? (Lesson 7.7)

   ○ $1.32    ○ $1.53
   ○ $1.77    ○ $3.21

4. Which of the following is true?
   (Lesson 2.12)

   ○ 185 = 581
   ○ 167 = 176
   ○ 273 > 304
   ○ 260 < 362

5. What number is shown with these blocks? (Lesson 2.3)

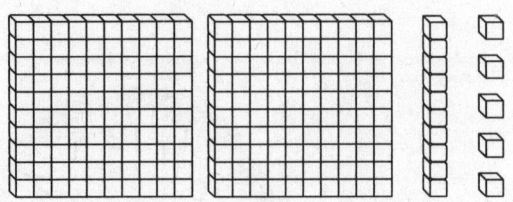

   ○ 215     ○ 251
   ○ 512     ○ 521

6. Which of these numbers is an even number? (Lesson 1.1)

   ○ 1
   ○ 3
   ○ 4
   ○ 5

Name _____

**Lesson 7.9**

# Time to 5 Minutes

COMMON CORE STANDARD CC.2.MD.7
Work with time and money.

**Look at the clock hands. Write the time.**

1.

2.

3.

4.

5.

6.

## PROBLEM SOLVING REAL WORLD

Draw the minute hand to show the time. Then write the time.

7. My hour hand points between the 4 and the 5. My minute hand points to the 9. What time do I show?

Chapter 7

one hundred seventy-three **P173**

## Lesson Check (CC.2.MD.7)

1. What is the time on this clock?

- ○ 8:05
- ○ 8:01
- ○ 1:40
- ○ 1:08

2. What is the time on this clock?

- ○ 4:07
- ○ 4:35
- ○ 7:20
- ○ 7:30

## Spiral Review (CC.2.OA.1, CC.2.OA.2, CC.2.OA.4, CC.2.NBT.1a, CC.2.NBT.1b)

3. What is the sum of $1 + 6 + 8$?
   (Lesson 3.4)

   - ○ 16
   - ○ 15
   - ○ 13
   - ○ 11

4. Which number has the same value as 30 tens? (Lesson 2.1)

   - ○ 3
   - ○ 30
   - ○ 300
   - ○ 3010

5. Steven has 3 rows of toys. There are 4 toys in each row. How many toys are there in all?
   (Lesson 3.11)

   - ○ 4
   - ○ 7
   - ○ 8
   - ○ 12

6. Jill has 14 buttons. She buys 8 more buttons. How many buttons does Jill have in all?
   (Lesson 3.8)

   - ○ 22
   - ○ 20
   - ○ 12
   - ○ 6

Name _____

# Practice Telling Time

**Lesson 7.10**

COMMON CORE STANDARD CC.2.MD.7
Work with time and money.

**Draw the minute hand to show the time. Write the time.**

1. quarter past 7

2. half past 3

3. 50 minutes after 1

4. quarter past 11

5. 15 minutes after 8

6. 5 minutes after 6

## PROBLEM SOLVING REAL WORLD

Draw a minute hand on the clock to solve.

7. Josh got to school at half past 8. Show this time on the clock.

Chapter 7

one hundred seventy-five **P175**

## Lesson Check (CC.2.MD.7)

1. What is the time on this clock?

   ○ quarter past 3
   ○ 6 minutes after 3
   ○ quarter past 6
   ○ half past 6

## Spiral Review (CC.2.OA.4, CC.2.NBT.3, CC.2.MD.7, CC.2.MD.8)

2. What is the value of this group of coins? (Lesson 7.3)

   ○ 21¢
   ○ 26¢
   ○ 31¢
   ○ 46¢

3. What time is shown on this clock? (Lesson 7.9)

   ○ 8:05
   ○ 7:15
   ○ 4:13
   ○ 3:35

4. Which is another way to write 647? (Lesson 2.6)

   ○ six hundred forty-seven
   ○ 60 + 40 + 7
   ○ 4 hundreds 6 tens 7 ones
   ○ 674

**Lesson 7.11**

Name _____

# A.M. and P.M.

**COMMON CORE STANDARD CC.2.MD.7**
Work with time and money.

Write the time. Then circle A.M. or P.M.

1. walk the dog

A.M.
P.M.

2. finish breakfast

A.M.
P.M.

3. put on pajamas

A.M.
P.M.

4. read a bedtime story

A.M.
P.M.

## PROBLEM SOLVING

Use the list of times. Complete the story.

5. Jess woke up at _____. She got on the bus at _____ and went to school. She left school at _____.

| 3:15 P.M. |
| 8:30 A.M. |
| 7:00 A.M. |

Chapter 7      one hundred seventy-seven **P177**

## Lesson Check (CC.2.MD.7)

1. The clock shows when the soccer game ended. What time was it?

    ○ 4:50 A.M.
    ○ 10:20 A.M.
    ○ 4:50 P.M.
    ○ 10:20 P.M.

2. The clock shows when Dad gets up for work. What time is it?

    ○ 2:30 A.M.
    ○ 6:10 A.M.
    ○ 2:30 P.M.
    ○ 6:10 P.M.

## Spiral Review (CC.2.NBT.3, CC.2.NBT.7, CC.2.MD.7, CC.2.MD.8)

3. Which coin has the same value as 25 pennies? (Lesson 7.2)

    ○ penny
    ○ nickel
    ○ dime
    ○ quarter

4. Which of these is another way to describe 72? (Lesson 1.4)

    ○ 7 + 2
    ○ 20 + 7
    ○ 70 + 2
    ○ 70 + 20

5. What is the sum? (Lesson 6.3)

    $$\begin{array}{r} 437 \\ +\phantom{0}24 \\ \hline \end{array}$$

    ○ 461
    ○ 451
    ○ 431
    ○ 413

6. Which time is quarter past 3? (Lesson 7.10)

    ○ 3:45
    ○ 3:15
    ○ 3:30
    ○ 2:45

P178 one hundred seventy-eight

Name _____

COMMON CORE STANDARDS CC.2.MD.7, CC.2.MD.8

# Chapter 7 Extra Practice

## Lessons 7.1–7.2 (pp. 337–344)
Count on to find the total value.

1.
   total value

2.
   total value

## Lesson 7.3 (pp. 345–348)
Draw and label the coins from greatest to least value. Find the total value.

1.

   _____

## Lesson 7.4 (pp. 349–352)
Use coins. Show the amount in two ways.
Draw and label the coins.

1.

Chapter 7     one hundred seventy-nine   P179

# Lesson 7.5 (pp. 353–355)
Circle coins to make $1.00.
Cross out the coins you do not use.

1.

# Lessons 7.8 – 7.9 (pp. 365–372)
Look at the clock hands. Write the time.

1.

2.

3.

4.

5.

6.

# Chapter 8

## School-Home Letter

### Dear Family,

My class started Chapter 8 this week. In this chapter, I will learn about inches and feet. I will also learn about measuring tools and showing measurement data.

Love, _____

### Vocabulary

**inch** Unit of length

**foot** 12 inches

**yardstick** A tool that shows 3 feet

### Home Activity

Record each family member's height with masking tape in a doorway of your house. Measure the height in inches. Write each person's name and height on the tape.

### Literature

Reading math stories reinforces ideas. Look for these books at the library.

**Measuring Penny** by Loreen Leedy. Henry Holt and Company, 1998.

**Twelve Snails to One Lizard** by Susan Hightower. Simon & Schuster, 1997.

# Capítulo 8
## Carta para la casa

### Querida familia:

Mi clase comenzó el Capítulo 8 esta semana. En este capítulo, aprenderé acerca de pulgadas y pies. También aprenderé sobre herramientas para medir y mostrar información sobre medidas.

Con cariño, _____

### Vocabulario

**pulgada** Unidad de longitud

**pie** 12 pulgadas

**regla de 1 yarda** Una herramienta con marcas que mostra 3 pies

### Actividad para la casa

En el marco de una puerta, marque con cinta adhesiva la altura de cada miembro de la familia. Mida la altura en pulgadas. Escriba el nombre de cada persona y su altura en la cinta adhesiva.

### Literatura

La lectura de cuentos matemáticos refuerza las ideas. Busque estos libros en la biblioteca.

**Measuring Penny** por Loreen Leedy. Henry Holt and Company, 1998.

**Twelve Snails to One Lizard** por Susan Hightower. Simon & Schuster, 1997.

Name _____

# Measure with Inch Models

**HANDS ON
Lesson 8.1**

**COMMON CORE STANDARD CC.2.MD.1**
Measure and estimate lengths in standard units.

**Use color tiles. Measure the length of the object in inches.**

1.

   about _____ inches

2.

   about _____ inches

3.

   about _____ inches

4.

   about _____ inches

**PROBLEM SOLVING**

5. Look around your classroom.
   Find an object that is about 4 inches long.
   Draw and label the object.

Chapter 8

## Lesson Check (CC.2.MD.1)

1. Jessie used color tiles to measure the rope. Which is the best choice for the length of the rope?

   ○ about 1 inch
   ○ about 2 inches
   ○ about 3 inches
   ○ about 4 inches

## Spiral Review (CC.2.NBT.5, CC.2.MD.7, CC.2.MD.8)

2. Adam has these coins. How much money is this? (Lesson 7.1)

   ○ 5¢
   ○ 20¢
   ○ 25¢
   ○ 40¢

3. Look at the clock hands. What time does this clock show? (Lesson 7.8)

   ○ 4:30
   ○ 5:00
   ○ 5:30
   ○ 6:00

4. What is the sum? (Lesson 4.7)

   $$\begin{array}{r}84\\+71\\\hline\end{array}$$

   ○ 165
   ○ 155
   ○ 53
   ○ 13

Name _____

# Make and Use a Ruler

**HANDS ON
Lesson 8.2**

**COMMON CORE STANDARD** CC.2.MD.1
Measure and estimate lengths in standard units.

**Measure the length with your ruler.
Count the inches.**

1.

about _____ inches

2.

about _____ inches

3.

about _____ inches

4.

about _____ inches

## PROBLEM SOLVING REAL WORLD

5. Use your ruler. Measure the width of this page in inches.

about _____ inches

Chapter 8 — one hundred eighty-five **P185**

# Lesson Check (CC.2.MD.1)

1. Use your ruler. What is the best choice for the length of this ribbon?

- ○ about 5 inches
- ○ about 4 inches
- ○ about 3 inches
- ○ about 2 inches

# Spiral Review (CC.2.OA.4, CC.2.NBT.7, CC.2.MD.7, CC.2.MD.8)

2. What time is shown on this clock? (Lesson 7.9)

   - ○ 9:15
   - ○ 4:45
   - ○ 3:45
   - ○ 3:09

3. What is the total value of these coins? (Lesson 7.2)

   - ○ 60¢
   - ○ 55¢
   - ○ 50¢
   - ○ 35¢

4. The first group collected 238 cans. The second group collected 345 cans. How many cans did the two groups collect?

   (Lesson 6.3)

   - ○ 107
   - ○ 573
   - ○ 583
   - ○ 585

5. There are 2 children in each row. How many children are in 5 rows? (Lesson 3.10)

   - ○ 3
   - ○ 5
   - ○ 7
   - ○ 10

Name _____

# Estimate Lengths in Inches

**Lesson 8.3**

**COMMON CORE STANDARD** CC.2.MD.3
Measure and estimate lengths in standard units.

The bead is 1 inch long.
Circle the best estimate for the length
of the string.

1.

   1 inch      4 inches      7 inches

2.

   3 inches      6 inches      9 inches

3.

   2 inches      3 inches      6 inches

4.

   2 inches      5 inches      8 inches

**PROBLEM SOLVING**

Solve. Write or draw to explain.

5. Ashley has some beads. Each bead is 2 inches long. How many beads will fit on a string that is 8 inches long?

   _____ beads

Chapter 8      one hundred eighty-seven    **P187**

## Lesson Check (CC.2.MD.3)

1. The bead is 1 inch long. Which is the best estimate for the length of the string?

- ○ 1 inch
- ○ 3 inches
- ○ 5 inches
- ○ 7 inches

## Spiral Review (CC.2.OA.1, CC.2.NBT.6, CC.2.MD.7)

2. Which clock shows 5 minutes after 6? (Lesson 7.10)

○          ○          ○          ○

3. Ella read 16 pages of her book on Monday and 26 pages on Tuesday. There are 64 pages in the book. How many more pages are left for Ella to read?

   (Lesson 5.11)

   - ○ 106
   - ○ 34
   - ○ 32
   - ○ 22

4. What is the sum? (Lesson 4.2)

   38 + 24 = _____

   - ○ 54
   - ○ 60
   - ○ 62
   - ○ 66

Name _____

# Measure with an Inch Ruler

**HANDS ON
Lesson 8.4**

**COMMON CORE STANDARD CC.2.MD.1**
Measure and estimate lengths in standard units.

**Measure the length to the nearest inch.**

1.

    _____ inches

2.

    _____ inches

3.

    _____ inches

4.

    _____ inches

**PROBLEM SOLVING** REAL WORLD

5. Measure the string. What is its total length?

    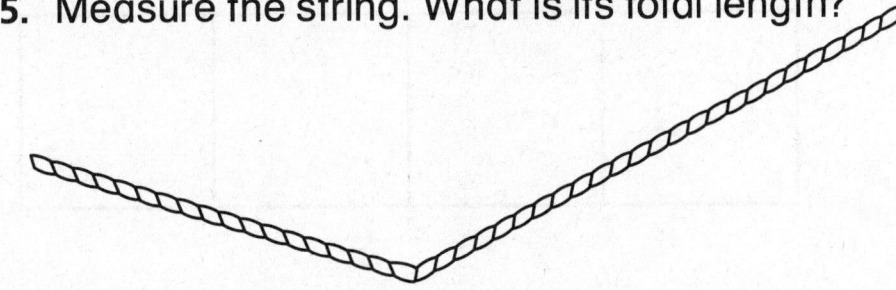

    _____ inches

Chapter 8      one hundred eighty-nine **P189**

# Lesson Check (CC.2.MD.1)

1. Use an inch ruler. What is the length to the nearest inch?

   ▭▭▭▭▭

   - ○ 1 inch
   - ○ 2 inches
   - ○ 3 inches
   - ○ 4 inches

2. Use an inch ruler. What is the length to the nearest inch?

   - ○ 2 inches
   - ○ 3 inches
   - ○ 4 inches
   - ○ 5 inches

# Spiral Review (CC.2.OA.2, CC.2.MD.1, CC.2.MD.7)

3. The clock shows the time that Jen got to school. What time did Jen get to school? (Lesson 7.11)
   - ○ 6:30 A.M.
   - ○ 8:30 A.M.
   - ○ 6:30 P.M.
   - ○ 8:30 P.M.

4. What is the difference? (Lesson 3.7)

   $13 - 5 = $ _____

   - ○ 18
   - ○ 10
   - ○ 9
   - ○ 8

5. Each color tile is about 1 inch long. Which is the best choice for the length of the ribbon? (Lesson 8.1)
   - ○ about 1 inch
   - ○ about 2 inches
   - ○ about 3 inches
   - ○ about 4 inches

P190 one hundred ninety

Name _____

# Problem Solving • Add and Subtract in Inches

**PROBLEM SOLVING**
**Lesson 8.5**

COMMON CORE STANDARDS CC.2.MD.5, CC.2.MD.6
Relate addition and subtraction to length.

**Draw a diagram. Write a number sentence using a ■ for the missing number. Solve.**

1. Molly had a ribbon that was 23 inches long. She cut 7 inches off the ribbon. How long is her ribbon now?

_____

Molly's ribbon is _____ inches long now.

2. Jed has a paper clip chain that is 11 inches long. He adds 7 inches of paper clips to the chain. How long is the paper clip chain now?

_____

The paper clip chain is _____ inches long now.

Chapter 8            one hundred ninety-one **P191**

# Lesson Check (CC.2.MD.5, CC.2.MD.6)

1. Allie has two pieces of string. Each one is 8 inches long. How many inches of string does she have altogether?

   ○ 16 inches   ○ 14 inches
   ○ 15 inches   ○ 12 inches

2. Jeff has a cube train that is 26 inches long. He removes 12 inches of cubes from the train. How long is Jeff's cube train now?

   ○ 38 inches   ○ 14 inches
   ○ 18 inches   ○ 12 inches

# Spiral Review (CC.2.MD.1, CC.2.MD.8)

3. Ann buys a pencil that costs 45¢. Which group of coins has a total value of 45¢? (Lesson 7.4)

   ○ 1 quarter and 1 dime
   ○ 1 quarter and 2 dimes
   ○ 2 quarters
   ○ 6 nickels and 1 dime

4. Use an inch ruler. What is the best choice for the length of this string? (Lesson 8.4)

   ○ about 1 inch
   ○ about 2 inches
   ○ about 3 inches
   ○ about 4 inches

5. Jason has these coins in a jar. What is the total value of these coins? (Lesson 7.3)

   ○ 30¢
   ○ 45¢
   ○ 50¢
   ○ 55¢

P192 one hundred ninety-two

Name _____

# Measure in Inches and Feet

**HANDS ON**
**Lesson 8.6**

**COMMON CORE STANDARD** CC.2.MD.2
Measure and estimate lengths in standard units.

Measure to the nearest inch.
Then measure to the nearest foot.

| Find the real object. | Measure. |
|---|---|
| 1. bookcase | _____ inches <br><br> _____ feet |
| 2. window | _____ inches <br><br> _____ feet |
| 3. chair | _____ inches <br><br> _____ feet |

## PROBLEM SOLVING REAL WORLD

4. Jake has a piece of yarn that is 4 feet long.
   Blair has a piece of yarn that is 4 inches long.
   Who has the longer piece of yarn? Explain.

   _____

   _____

Chapter 8      one hundred ninety-three **P193**

# Lesson Check (CC.2.MD.2)

1. Larry is telling his sister about using a ruler to measure length. Which sentence is true?
   - ○ 1 foot is shorter than 1 inch.
   - ○ 1 foot is longer than 1 inch.
   - ○ 1 inch is longer than 1 foot.
   - ○ 1 foot is the same length as 1 inch.

# Spiral Review (CC.2.NBT.5, CC.2.NBT.7, CC.2.MD.7, CC.2.MD.8)

2. Matt put this money in his pocket. What is the total value of this money? (Lesson 7.6)

   - ○ $1.01
   - ○ $1.06
   - ○ $1.10
   - ○ $1.11

3. What time is shown on this clock? (Lesson 7.9)

   - ○ 12:50    ○ 1:50
   - ○ 10:05    ○ 1:10

4. Ali had 38 game cards. Her friend gave her 15 more game cards. How many game cards does Ali have now? (Lesson 4.7)
   - ○ 53
   - ○ 48
   - ○ 43
   - ○ 23

Name _____

## Estimate Lengths in Feet

**Lesson 8.7**

**COMMON CORE STANDARD CC.2.MD.3**
Measure and estimate lengths in standard units.

Find each object.
Estimate how many 12-inch rulers will be about the same length as the object.

1. door

   Estimate: _____ rulers, or _____ feet

2. flag

   Estimate: _____ rulers, or _____ feet

3. wall of a small room

   Estimate: _____ rulers, or _____ feet

**PROBLEM SOLVING**  REAL WORLD

Solve. Write or draw to explain.

4. Mr. and Mrs. Baker place 12-inch rulers along the length of a rug. They each line up 3 rulers along the edge of the rug. What is the length of the rug?

about _____ feet

Chapter 8

one hundred ninety-five **P195**

# Lesson Check (CC.2.MD.3)

1. Which is the best estimate for the length of a bike?
   - ○ 1 foot
   - ○ 2 feet
   - ○ 5 feet
   - ○ 9 feet

2. Which is the best estimate for the length of a football?
   - ○ 1 foot
   - ○ 4 feet
   - ○ 5 feet
   - ○ 8 feet

# Spiral Review (CC.2.NBT.5, CC.2.NBT.7, CC.2.MD.8)

3. Which group of coins has a value of $1.00? (Lesson 7.5)
   - ○ 2 quarters, 2 dimes, 3 nickels
   - ○ 2 quarters, 3 dimes, 4 nickels
   - ○ 2 quarters, 4 dimes, 3 nickels
   - ○ 3 quarters, 2 dimes, 2 nickels

4. Which group of coins has a total value of 37¢? (Lesson 7.4)
   - ○ 3 nickels, 7 pennies
   - ○ 1 quarter, 2 dimes, 1 nickel
   - ○ 2 dimes, 3 nickels, 2 pennies
   - ○ 7 quarters, 3 dimes

5. There are 68 children in the school. There are 19 children on the playground. How many more children are in the school than on the playground? (Lesson 5.2)
   - ○ 87
   - ○ 79
   - ○ 49
   - ○ 47

6. What is the sum? (Lesson 6.3)

   $$\begin{array}{r} 548 \\ + 436 \\ \hline \end{array}$$

   - ○ 112
   - ○ 912
   - ○ 974
   - ○ 984

P196 one hundred ninety-six

Name _____

## Choose a Tool

**Lesson 8.8**

COMMON CORE STANDARD CC.2.MD.1
Measure and estimate lengths in standard units.

Choose the best tool for measuring the real object. Then measure and record the length or distance.

inch ruler
yardstick
measuring tape

1. the length of your desk

Tool: _____

Length: _____

2. the distance around a basket

Tool: _____

Length: _____

## PROBLEM SOLVING REAL WORLD

Choose the better tool for measuring.
Explain your choice.

3. Mark wants to measure the length of his room. Should he use an inch ruler or a yardstick?

Mark should use _____ because _____

_____

Chapter 8     one hundred ninety-seven **P197**

# Lesson Check (CC.2.MD.1)

1. Kim wants to measure the distance around her bike tire. Which is the best tool for her to use?

    ○ cup
    ○ yardstick
    ○ color tiles
    ○ measuring tape

2. Ben wants to measure the length of a seesaw. Which is the best tool for him to use?

    ○ cup
    ○ yardstick
    ○ color tiles
    ○ paper clips

# Spiral Review (CC.2.MD.2, CC.2.MD.3, CC.2.MD.5, CC.2.MD.6)

3. Which is the best estimate for the length of a sheet of paper? (Lesson 8.7)

    ○ 1 foot
    ○ 3 feet
    ○ 6 feet
    ○ 10 feet

4. Andy has a rope that is 24 inches long. He cuts off 7 inches from the rope. How long is the rope now? (Lesson 8.5)

    ○ 20 inches
    ○ 17 inches
    ○ 15 inches
    ○ 9 inches

5. Jan is telling her friend about using a ruler to measure length. Which sentence is true? (Lesson 8.6)

    ○ 3 inches is longer than 1 foot.
    ○ 1 foot is shorter than 3 inches.
    ○ 1 foot is longer than 12 inches.
    ○ 12 inches is the same length as 1 foot.

Name _____

## Display Measurement Data

**Lesson 8.9**

COMMON CORE STANDARD CC.2.MD.9
Represent and interpret data.

1. Use an inch ruler. Measure and record the lengths of 4 different books in inches.

   | 1st book: _____ inches |
   |---|
   | 2nd book: _____ inches |
   | 3rd book: _____ inches |
   | 4th book: _____ inches |

2. Make a line plot of the information above. Write a title for a line plot. Then write the numbers and draw the **X**s.

### PROBLEM SOLVING REAL WORLD

3. Jesse measured the lengths of some strings. Use his list to complete the line plot.

   | Lengths of Strings |
   |---|
   | 5 inches |
   | 7 inches |
   | 6 inches |
   | 8 inches |
   | 5 inches |

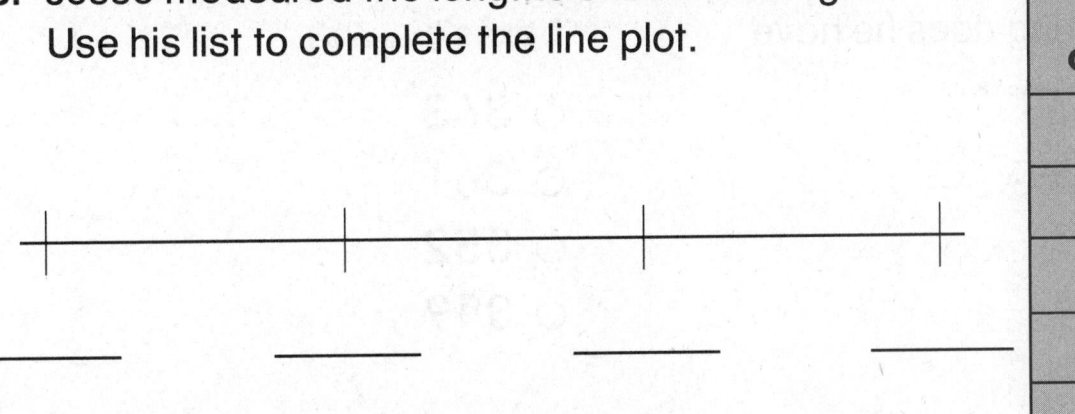

Chapter 8

# Lesson Check (CC.2.MD.9)

1. Use the line plot. How many sticks are 4 inches long?

   ○ 4
   ○ 3
   ○ 2
   ○ 1

Lengths of Sticks in Inches

# Spiral Review (CC.2.NBT.7, CC.2.MD.1, CC.2.MD.3, CC.2.MD.5, CC.2.MD.6)

2. Kim wants to measure a ball. Which is the best tool for Kim to use? (Lesson 8.8)

   ○ counter
   ○ pencil
   ○ paper clip
   ○ measuring tape

3. Which is the best estimate for the length of a teacher's desk? (Lesson 8.7)

   ○ 20 feet
   ○ 15 feet
   ○ 5 feet
   ○ 1 foot

4. Kurt has a string that is 12 inches long and another string that is 5 inches long. How many inches of string does he have altogether? (Lesson 8.5)

   ○ 7 inches
   ○ 12 inches
   ○ 17 inches
   ○ 19 inches

5. One box has 147 books. The other box has 216 books. How many books are there in both boxes? (Lesson 6.3)

   ○ 363
   ○ 361
   ○ 352
   ○ 349

Name _____

COMMON CORE STANDARDS CC.2.MD.1, CC.2.MD.2, CC.2.MD.3, CC.2.MD.9

# Chapter 8 Extra Practice

**Lesson 8.1** (pp. 389–392)
Use color tiles. Measure the length of the object in inches.

1.

about ____ inches

**Lesson 8.3** (pp. 397–400)
The bead is 1 inch long. Circle the best estimate for the length of the string.

1.

    3 inches      5 inches      7 inches

**Lesson 8.4** (pp. 401–404)
Measure the length to the nearest inch.

1.

____ inches

**Lesson 8.6** (pp. 409–412)
Measure to the nearest inch.
Then measure to the nearest foot.

| Find the real object. | Measure. |
|---|---|
| 1. chair | ____ inches <br> ____ feet |

Chapter 8      two hundred one **P201**

# Lesson 8.7 (pp. 413–416)

Find the object. Estimate how many 12-inch rulers will be about the same length as the object.

1. table

Estimate: _____ rulers, or _____ feet

# Lesson 8.8 (pp. 417–420)

Choose the best tool for measuring the real object. Then measure and record the length.

> inch ruler
> yardstick
> measuring tape

1. the length of a door

Tool: _____

Length: _____

# Lesson 8.9 (pp. 421–424)

1. Use an inch ruler. Measure and record the lengths of 4 pencils in inches.

2. Write a title for the line plot. Then write the numbers and draw the Xs.

| 1st pencil: _____ inches |
| 2nd pencil: _____ inches |
| 3rd pencil: _____ inches |
| 4th pencil: _____ inches |

# Chapter 9

## School-Home Letter

**Dear Family,**

My class started Chapter 9 this week. In this chapter, I will learn how to measure using centimeters and meters. I will also solve problems about adding and subtracting lengths.

Love, _____

### Vocabulary

**centimeter** Unit of length

**meter** 100 centimeters

### Home Activity

Show your child an object that is about ten centimeters long. Have your child choose three or four more objects and estimate each length as more than ten centimeters or less than ten centimeters. Use the object that is about ten centimeters long to check your child's estimates.

### Literature

Reading math stories reinforces ideas. Look for these books at the library.

*How Tall, How Short, How Far Away?* by David Adler. Holiday House, 2000.

*Length* by Henry Arthur Pluckrose. Children's Press, 1995.

# Capítulo 9
## Carta para la casa

### Querida familia:
Mi clase comenzó el Capítulo 9 esta semana. En este capítulo, aprenderé a medir usando centímetros y metros. También resolveré problemas de suma y resta de longitudes.

Con cariño, _____

### Vocabulario

**centímetro** unidad de longitud

**metro** 100 centímetros

### Actividad para la casa
Muéstrele a su hijo un objeto de unos diez centímetros de largo. Pídale que elija tres o cuatro objetos más y que estime el largo de cada uno en más de diez centímetros o en menos de diez centímetros. Use el objeto de unos diezcentímetros de largo para comprobar las estimaciones de su hijo.

### Literatura
Leer cuentos de matemáticas refuerza los conceptos. Busque estos libros en la biblioteca.

**How Tall, How Short, How Far Away?**
por David Adler.
Holiday House, 2000.

**Length**
por Henry Arthur Pluckrose.
Children's Press, 1995.

Name _____

# Measure with a Centimeter Model

**HANDS ON
Lesson 9.1**

**COMMON CORE STANDARD** CC.2.MD.1
Measure and estimate lengths in standard units.

**Use a unit cube. Measure the length in centimeters.**

1.

   about _____ centimeters

2.

   about _____ centimeters

3.

   about _____ centimeters

4.

   about _____ centimeters

**PROBLEM SOLVING** REAL WORLD

Solve. Write or draw to explain.

5. Susan has a pencil that is 3 centimeters shorter than this string. How long is the pencil?

   about _____ centimeters

Chapter 9 • two hundred five **P205**

# Lesson Check (CC.2.MD.1)

1. Sarah used unit cubes to measure the length of a ribbon. Which is the best choice for the length of the ribbon?

- ○ 1 centimeter
- ○ 6 centimeters
- ○ 4 centimeters
- ○ 10 centimeters

# Spiral Review (CC.2.MD.5, CC.2.MD.6, CC.2.MD.7)

2. What is the time on this clock?
   (Lesson 7.8)

   - ○ 12:00
   - ○ 10:00
   - ○ 11:00
   - ○ 9:00

3. What is the time on this clock?
   (Lesson 7.9)

   - ○ 8:20
   - ○ 5:08
   - ○ 5:40
   - ○ 4:40

4. Dan has a paper strip that is 28 inches long. He tears 6 inches off the strip. How long is the paper strip now? (Lesson 8.5)

   - ○ 16 inches
   - ○ 28 inches
   - ○ 22 inches
   - ○ 34 inches

5. Rita has 1 quarter, 1 dime, and 2 pennies. What is the total value of Rita's coins? (Lesson 7.3)

   - ○ 41¢
   - ○ 26¢
   - ○ 37¢
   - ○ 17¢

Name _____

# Estimate Lengths in Centimeters

**Lesson 9.2**

**COMMON CORE STANDARD CC.2.MD.3**
Measure and estimate lengths in standard units.

1. The toothpick is about 6 centimeters long. Circle the best estimate for the length of the yarn.

   6 centimeters

   9 centimeters

   12 centimeters

2. The pen is about 11 centimeters long. Circle the best estimate for the length of the eraser.

   4 centimeters

   10 centimeters

   14 centimeters

3. The string is about 6 centimeters long. Circle the best estimate for the length of the crayon.

   5 centimeters

   9 centimeters

   14 centimeters

## PROBLEM SOLVING

4. The string is about 6 centimeters long. Draw a pencil that is about 12 centimeters long.

Chapter 9

two hundred seven **P207**

## Lesson Check (CC.2.MD.3)

1. The pencil is about 12 centimeters long. Which is the best estimate for the length of the yarn?

   ○ 5 centimeters     ○ 12 centimeters
   ○ 10 centimeters    ○ 24 centimeters

## Spiral Review (CC.2.NBT.5, CC.2.MD.5, CC.2.MD.6, CC.2.MD.8)

2. What is the difference? (Lesson 5.5)

   58
   − 23
   ___

   ○ 35
   ○ 53
   ○ 62
   ○ 81

3. What is the sum? (Lesson 4.8)

   14 + 65

   ○ 42
   ○ 51
   ○ 54
   ○ 79

4. Adrian has a cube train that is 13 inches long. He adds 6 inches of cubes to the train. How long is the cube train now? (Lesson 8.5)

   ○ 7 inches
   ○ 11 inches
   ○ 19 inches
   ○ 27 inches

5. What is the total value of this group of coins? (Lesson 7.1)

   ○ 8¢
   ○ 17¢
   ○ 22¢
   ○ 26¢

P208 two hundred eight

Name _____

# Measure with a Centimeter Ruler

**HANDS ON
Lesson 9.3**

**COMMON CORE STANDARD CC.2.MD.1**
Measure and estimate lengths in standard units.

**Measure the length to the nearest centimeter.**

1.

   _____ centimeters

2.

   _____ centimeters

3. 

   _____ centimeters

## PROBLEM SOLVING

4. Draw a string that is about 8 centimeters long. Then use a centimeter ruler to check the length.

Chapter 9 two hundred nine **P209**

# Lesson Check (CC.2.MD.1)

1. Use a centimeter ruler. What is the length of this pencil to the nearest centimeter?

- ○ 5 centimeters
- ○ 6 centimeters
- ○ 10 centimeters
- ○ 12 centimeters

# Spiral Review (CC.2.MD.7, CC.2.MD.8, CC.2.MD.9)

2. What is the time on this clock?

   (Lesson 7.9)

   - ○ 1:20
   - ○ 2:04
   - ○ 3:25
   - ○ 4:05

3. What is the total value of this group of coins? (Lesson 7.1)

   - ○ 16¢
   - ○ 21¢
   - ○ 35¢
   - ○ 57¢

4. Use the line plot. How many pencils are 5 inches long?

   (Lesson 8.9)

   - ○ 7
   - ○ 5
   - ○ 2
   - ○ 1

   **Lengths of Pencils in Inches**

Name _____

# Problem Solving • Add and Subtract Lengths

**PROBLEM SOLVING
Lesson 9.4**

COMMON CORE STANDARDS CC.2.MD.6, CC.2.MD.5
Relate addition and subtraction to length.

**Draw a diagram. Write a number sentence using a ▢ for the missing number. Then solve.**

1. A straw is 20 centimeters long. Mr. Jones cuts off 8 centimeters of the straw. How long is the straw now?

_____

The straw is _____ centimeters long now.

2. Ella has a piece of blue yarn that is 14 centimeters long. She has a piece of red yarn that is 9 centimeters long. How many centimeters of yarn does she have altogether?

_____

She has _____ centimeters of yarn altogether.

Chapter 9 two hundred eleven **P211**

# Lesson Check (CC.2.MD.6, CC.2.MD.5)

1. Tina has a paper clip chain that is 25 centimeters long. She takes off 8 centimeters of the chain. How long is the chain now?

- ○ 13 centimeters
- ○ 17 centimeters
- ○ 23 centimeters
- ○ 33 centimeters

# Spiral Review (CC.2.NBT.7, CC.2.MD.7, CC.2.MD.8)

2. What is the sum? (Lesson 6.3)

    327
  + 145

   - ○ 182
   - ○ 262
   - ○ 462
   - ○ 472

3. Which is another way to write the time half past 7? (Lesson 7.10)

   - ○ 6:30
   - ○ 7:05
   - ○ 7:30
   - ○ 8:15

4. Molly has these coins in her pocket. How much money does she have in her pocket? (Lesson 7.2)

- ○ 75¢
- ○ 70¢
- ○ 65¢
- ○ 55¢

Name _____

# Centimeters and Meters

**HANDS ON Lesson 9.5**

**COMMON CORE STANDARD CC.2.MD.2**
Measure and estimate lengths in standard units.

Measure to the nearest centimeter.
Then measure to the nearest meter.

| Find the real object. | Measure. |
|---|---|
| 1. bookcase | _____ centimeters <br> _____ meters |
| 2. window | _____ centimeters <br> _____ meters |
| 3. map | _____ centimeters <br> _____ meters |

## PROBLEM SOLVING

4. Sally will measure the length of a wall in both centimeters and meters. Will there be fewer centimeters or fewer meters? Explain.

_____

_____

_____

Chapter 9     two hundred thirteen **P213**

## Lesson Check (CC.2.MD.2)

1. Use a centimeter ruler. Which is the best choice for the length of the toothbrush?

- ○ 4 centimeters
- ○ 14 centimeters
- ○ 20 centimeters
- ○ 25 centimeters

## Spiral Review (CC.2.NBT.7, CC.2.MD.2, CC.2.MD.8)

2. Which group of coins has a total value of 65¢? (Lesson 7.4)

   - ○ 5 dimes and 3 nickels
   - ○ 50 pennies
   - ○ 1 quarter and 2 dimes
   - ○ 3 dimes and 7 pennies

3. Janet has a poster that is about 3 feet long. Which sentence is true? (Lesson 8.6)

   - ○ 3 feet is shorter than 12 inches.
   - ○ 3 feet is longer than 12 inches.
   - ○ 12 inches is as long as 3 feet.
   - ○ 12 inches is longer than 3 feet.

4. What is the sum? (Lesson 6.4)

   ```
     483
   + 162
   ```

   - ○ 321
   - ○ 421
   - ○ 545
   - ○ 645

5. Which group of coins has a value of $1.00? (Lesson 7.5)

   - ○ 4 dimes
   - ○ 3 quarters and 2 nickels
   - ○ 4 quarters
   - ○ 3 quarters and 3 dimes

P214 two hundred fourteen

Name _____

**Lesson 9.6**

## Estimate Lengths in Meters

**COMMON CORE STANDARD** CC.2.MD.3
Measure and estimate lengths in standard units.

**Find the real object.**
**Estimate its length in meters.**

1. poster

about _____ meters

2. chalkboard

about _____ meters

3. bookshelf

about _____ meters

### PROBLEM SOLVING REAL WORLD

4. Barbara and Luke each placed 2 meter sticks end-to-end along the length of a large table. About how long is the table?

about _____ meters

Chapter 9      two hundred fifteen **P215**

# Lesson Check (CC.2.MD.3)

1. Which is the best estimate for the length of a real baseball bat?

   - ○ 1 meter
   - ○ 3 meters
   - ○ 5 meters
   - ○ 7 meters

2. Which is the best estimate for the length of a real couch?

   - ○ 8 meters
   - ○ 6 meters
   - ○ 5 meters
   - ○ 2 meters

# Spiral Review (CC.2.MD.1, CC.2.MD.8)

3. Sara has two $1 bills, 3 quarters, and 1 dime. How much money does she have? (Lesson 7.7)

   - ○ $1.85
   - ○ $2.40
   - ○ $2.65
   - ○ $2.85

4. Use an inch ruler. What is the length of this straw to the nearest inch? (Lesson 8.2)

   - ○ 4 inches
   - ○ 3 inches
   - ○ 2 inches
   - ○ 1 inch

5. Scott has this money in his pocket. What is the total value of this money? (Lesson 7.6)

   - ○ $1.05
   - ○ $1.15
   - ○ $1.20
   - ○ $1.35

P216 two hundred sixteen

Name _____

# Measure and Compare Lengths

**HANDS ON**
**Lesson 9.7**

COMMON CORE STANDARD CC.2.MD.4
Measure and estimate lengths in standard units.

**Measure the length of each object. Write a number sentence to find the difference between the lengths.**

1.

   _____ centimeters

   _____ centimeters

   _____ − _____ = _____
   centimeters  centimeters  centimeters

   The craft stick is _____ centimeters longer than the chalk.

2.

   _____ centimeters

   _____ centimeters

   _____ − _____ = _____
   centimeters  centimeters  centimeters

   The string is _____ centimeters longer than the toothpick.

## PROBLEM SOLVING

Solve. Write or draw to explain.

3. A string is 11 centimeters long, a ribbon is 24 centimeters long, and a large paper clip is 5 centimeters long. How much longer is the ribbon than the string?

   _____ centimeters longer

Chapter 9                         two hundred seventeen  **P217**

# Lesson Check (CC.2.MD.4)

1. How much longer is the marker than the paper clip?

- ○ 11 centimeters longer
- ○ 10 centimeters longer
- ○ 8 centimeters longer
- ○ 5 centimeters longer

# Spiral Review (CC.2.MD.3, CC.2.MD.7, CC.2.MD.8)

2. What is the total value of these coins? (Lesson 7.3)

- ○ 41¢
- ○ 66¢
- ○ 75¢
- ○ 78¢

3. Which is the best estimate for the length of a real chalkboard?
(Lesson 8.7)
   - ○ 50 feet
   - ○ 7 feet
   - ○ 7 inches
   - ○ 1 inch

4. Cindy leaves at half past 2. At what time does Cindy leave?
(Lesson 7.10)
   - ○ 2:45
   - ○ 2:30
   - ○ 2:15
   - ○ 1:30

Name _____

COMMON CORE STANDARDS CC.2.MD.1, CC.2.MD.2, CC.2.MD.3, CC.2.MD.4

# Chapter 9 Extra Practice

### Lesson 9.1 (pp. 433–436)
Use a unit cube.
Measure the length in centimeters.

1.

   about _____ centimeters

2.

   about _____ centimeters

### Lesson 9.2 (pp. 437–440)

1. The leaf is about 6 centimeters long. Circle the best estimate for the length of the string.

   6 centimeters

   9 centimeters

   12 centimeters

### Lesson 9.3 (pp. 441–444)
Measure the length to the nearest centimeter.

1.

   _____ centimeters

2.

   _____ centimeters

Chapter 9     two hundred nineteen   **P219**

## Lesson 9.5 (pp. 449–452)

Measure to the nearest centimeter.
Then measure to the nearest meter.

| Find the real object. | Measure. |
|---|---|
| 1. poster | _____ centimeters<br><br>_____ meters |

## Lesson 9.6 (pp. 453–456)

Find the real object.
Estimate its length in meters.

1.

about _____ meters

## Lesson 9.7 (pp. 457–460)

Measure the length of each object. Write a number sentence to find the difference between the lengths.

1.

_____ centimeters

_____ centimeters

_____ − _____ = _____
centimeters  centimeters  centimeters

The pencil is _____ centimeters longer than the string.

P220 two hundred twenty

# Chapter 10

## School-Home Letter

**Dear Family,**

My class started Chapter 10 this week. In this chapter, I will learn about collecting data, making graphs, and interpreting the data.

Love, _____

### Vocabulary

**picture graph** A graph that uses pictures to show data

| Apples Sold | | | | |
|---|---|---|---|---|
| Eric | ● | ● | | |
| Deb | ● | ● | ● | ● |
| Alex | ● | | | |

Key: Each ● stands for 1 apple.

**bar graph** A graph that uses bars to show data

### Home Activity

Take your child on a walk in your neighborhood. Help your child make a tally chart to record how many people you see driving, walking, and biking. Then talk with your child about the information that is in your tally chart.

| How People Are Moving ||
|---|---|
| How Moving | Tally |
| driving | ||||  || |
| walking | |||| |
| biking | || |

### Literature

Reading math stories reinforces learning. Look for these books at the library.

**Tables and Graphs of Healthy Things** by Joan Freese. Gareth Stevens Publishing, 2008.

**Lemonade for Sale** by Stuart J. Murphy. Harper Collins, 1998.

# Capítulo 10
## Carta para la casa

### Querida familia:

Mi clase comenzó el Capítulo 10 esta semana. En este capítulo, aprenderé a recolectar datos, hacer grácas e interpretar datos.

Con cariño, _____

### Vocabulario

**pictografía** una gráfica que usa ilustraciones para mostrar datos

| Manzanas vendidas | |
|---|---|
| Eric | ● ● |
| Deb | ● ● ● ● |
| Alex | ● |

Clave: Cada ● representa 2 manzanas.

**gráfica de barras** una gráfica que usa barras para mostrar datos

### Actividad para la casa

Lleve a pasear a su hijo por el vecindario. Ayúdelo a crear una tabla de conteo para anotar cuántas personas ven manejando, caminando y montando en bicicleta. Luego, conversen sobre la información que hay en la tabla de conteo.

| Cómo se mueve la gente | |
|---|---|
| Se mueven | Conteo |
| manejando | ℍℍ ΙΙ |
| caminando | ΙΙΙΙ |
| en bicicleta | ΙΙ |

### Literatura

Leer cuentos de matemáticas refuerza los conceptos. Busque estos libros en la biblioteca.

**Table and Graphs of Healthy Things** por Joan Freese. Gareth Stevens Publishing, 2008.

**Lemonade for Sale** por Stuart J. Murphy. Harper Collins, 1998.

Name _____

## Collect Data

**Lesson 10.1**

COMMON CORE STANDARD CC.2.MD.10
Represent and interpret data.

1. Take a survey. Ask 10 classmates how they got to school. Use tally marks to show their choices.

| How We Got to School ||
|---|---|
| Way | Tally |
| walk | |
| bus | |
| car | |
| bike | |

_____

2. How many classmates rode in a bus to school?

_____ classmates

_____

3. How many classmates rode in a car to school?

_____ classmates

_____

4. In which way did the fewest classmates get to school?

_____

5. In which way did the most classmates get to school?

_____

6. Did more classmates get to school by walking or by riding in a car?

_____

How many more?

_____ more classmates

Chapter 10

two hundred twenty-three **P223**

# Lesson Check (CC.2.MD.10)

1. Use the tally chart. Which color did the fewest children choose?

   ○ blue
   ○ green
   ○ red
   ○ yellow

| Favorite Color | |
|---|---|
| Color | Tally |
| blue | ||| |
| green | |||| |||| |
| red | |||| || |
| yellow | |||| | |

# Spiral Review (CC.2.MD.5, CC.2.MD.6, CC.2.MD.7, CC.2.MD.8)

2. Which group of coins has a value of $1.00? (Lesson 7.5)

   ○ 10 pennies
   ○ 10 nickels
   ○ 10 dimes
   ○ 10 quarters

3. Jared has two ropes. Each rope is 9 inches long. How many inches of rope does he have in all? (Lesson 8.5)

   ○ 10 inches     ○ 18 inches
   ○ 16 inches     ○ 21 inches

4. The clock shows the time Lee got to school. At what time did she get to school? (Lesson 7.11)

   ○ 3:40 A.M.     ○ 3:40 P.M.
   ○ 8:15 A.M.     ○ 8:15 P.M.

5. Liza finished studying at half past 3. What time did Liza finish studying? (Lesson 7.10)

   ○ 3:30
   ○ 3:15
   ○ 2:45
   ○ 2:15

Name _____

## Read Picture Graphs

**Lesson 10.2**

**COMMON CORE STANDARD** CC.2.MD.10
Represent and interpret data.

Use the picture graph to answer the questions.

| Number of Books Read | | | | | | |
|---|---|---|---|---|---|---|
| Ryan | 📕 | 📕 | 📕 | 📕 | | |
| Gwen | 📕 | 📕 | | | | |
| Anna | 📕 | 📕 | 📕 | 📕 | 📕 | 📕 |
| Henry | 📕 | 📕 | 📕 | | | |

Key: Each 📕 stands for 1 book.

1. How many books in all did Henry and Anna read?  _____ books

2. How many more books did Ryan read than Gwen?  _____ more books

3. How many fewer books did Gwen read than Anna?  _____ fewer books

4. How many books did the four children read in all?  _____ books

## PROBLEM SOLVING REAL WORLD

Use the picture graph above. Write or draw to explain.

5. Carlos read 4 books. How many children read fewer books than Carlos?

_____ children

Chapter 10

# Lesson Check (CC.2.MD.10)

1. Use the picture graph. Who has the most fish?

   ○ Jane
   ○ Will
   ○ Gina
   ○ Evan

   | Our Fish | | | | | |
   |---|---|---|---|---|---|
   | Jane | 🐟 | | | | |
   | Will | 🐟 | 🐟 | 🐟 | | |
   | Gina | 🐟 | 🐟 | 🐟 | 🐟 | |
   | Evan | 🐟 | 🐟 | | | |

   Key: Each 🐟 stands for 1 fish.

# Spiral Review (CC.2.MD.1, CC.2.MD.7, CC.2.MD.8)

2. What is the time on this clock? (Lesson 7.9)

   ○ 1:55        ○ 3:05
   ○ 2:55        ○ 11:15

3. Each unit cube is about 1 centimeter long. Which is the best estimate for the length of the paper clip? (Lesson 9.1)

   ○ 1 centimeter
   ○ 3 centimeters
   ○ 4 centimeters
   ○ 8 centimeters

4. What is the total value of this group of coins? (Lesson 7.2)

   ○ 61¢        ○ 60¢        ○ 56¢        ○ 52¢

P226 two hundred twenty-six

Name _____

# Make Picture Graphs

**Lesson 10.3**

COMMON CORE STANDARD CC.2.MD.10
Represent and interpret data.

1. Use the tally chart to complete the picture graph. Draw a ☺ for each child.

**Favorite Cookie**

| Cookie | Tally |
|---|---|
| chocolate | III |
| oatmeal | I |
| peanut butter | 卌 |
| shortbread | IIII |

**Favorite Cookie**

| | | | | | |
|---|---|---|---|---|---|
| chocolate | | | | | |
| oatmeal | | | | | |
| peanut butter | | | | | |
| shortbread | | | | | |

Key: Each ☺ stands for 1 child.

2. How many children chose chocolate? _____ children

3. How many fewer children chose oatmeal than peanut butter? _____ fewer children

4. Which cookie did the most children choose?

   _____

5. How many children in all chose a favorite cookie? _____ children

6. How many children chose oatmeal or shortbread? _____ children

Chapter 10

two hundred twenty-seven **P227**

# Lesson Check (CC.2.MD.10)

1. Use the picture graph. How many more rainy days were there in April than in May?

| Number of Rainy Days | | | | | |
|---|---|---|---|---|---|
| March | ☂ | ☂ | ☂ | ☂ | ☂ |
| April | ☂ | ☂ | ☂ | ☂ | |
| May | ☂ | ☂ | | | |

Key: Each ☂ stands for 1 day.

- ○ 2
- ○ 4
- ○ 6
- ○ 12

# Spiral Review (CC.2.MD.1, CC.2.MD.8)

2. Rita has one $1 bill, 2 quarters, and 3 dimes. What is the total value of Rita's money? (Lesson 7.7)

- ○ $1.23
- ○ $1.35
- ○ $1.42
- ○ $1.80

3. Lucas put 4 quarters and 3 nickels into his coin bank. How much money did Lucas put into his coin bank? (Lesson 7.6)

- ○ $1.15
- ○ $1.25
- ○ $1.30
- ○ $1.75

4. Use a centimeter ruler. Which is the best choice for the length of this string? (Lesson 9.3)

- ○ 2 centimeters
- ○ 4 centimeters
- ○ 6 centimeters
- ○ 10 centimeters

5. What is the total value of this group of coins? (Lesson 7.1)

- ○ 8¢
- ○ 17¢
- ○ 21¢
- ○ 26¢

P228 two hundred twenty-eight

Name _____

Lesson **10.4**

**Read Bar Graphs**

COMMON CORE STANDARD CC.2.MD.10
Represent and interpret data.

Use the bar graph.

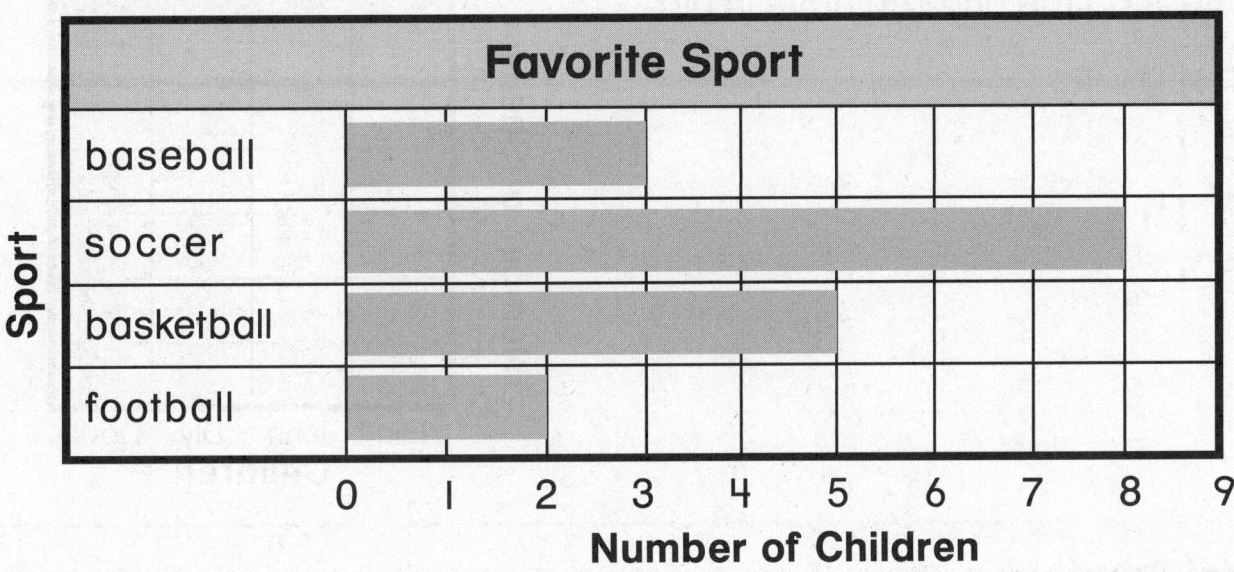

1. How many children chose basketball? _____ children

2. Which sport did the most children choose? _____

3. How many more children chose basketball than baseball? _____ more children

4. Which sport did the fewest children choose? _____

5. How many children chose a sport that was not soccer? _____ children

**PROBLEM SOLVING**

6. How many children chose baseball or basketball?

_____ children

Chapter 10

two hundred twenty-nine **P229**

# Lesson Check (CC.2.MD.10)

1. Use the bar graph. How many shells do the children have in all?

    ○ 10
    ○ 12
    ○ 14
    ○ 16

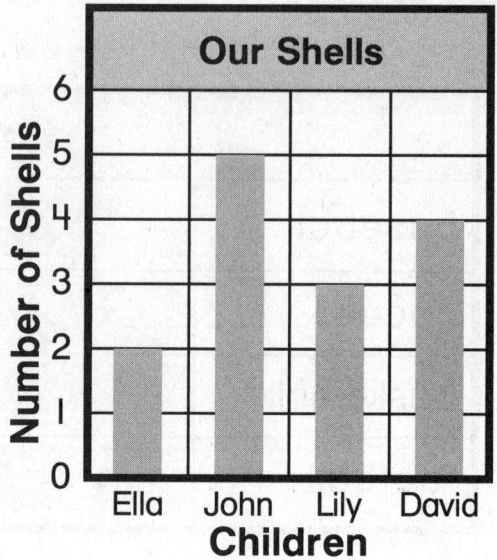

# Spiral Review (CC.2.MD.1, CC.2.MD.8, CC.2.MD.9)

2. Use the line plot. How many twigs are 3 inches long? (Lesson 8.9)

    ○ 8
    ○ 5
    ○ 4
    ○ 3

**Lengths of Twigs in Inches**

3. Use a centimeter ruler. Which is the best choice for the length of the yarn? (Lesson 9.3)

    ○ 7 centimeters
    ○ 4 centimeters
    ○ 2 centimeters
    ○ 1 centimeter

4. Noah buys a pencil. He uses 1 quarter and 2 nickels to pay. How much money does the pencil cost? (Lesson 7.4)

    ○ 45¢
    ○ 35¢
    ○ 30¢
    ○ 27¢

Name _____

# Make Bar Graphs

**Lesson 10.5**

COMMON CORE STANDARD CC.2.MD.10
Represent and interpret data.

Maria asked her friends how many hours they practice soccer each week.

- Jessie practices for 3 hours.
- Victor practices for 2 hours.
- Samantha practices for 5 hours.
- David practices for 6 hours.

1. Write a title and labels for the bar graph.

_____

2. Draw bars in the graph to show the data.

| _____ | | | | | | | | | | | |
|---|---|---|---|---|---|---|---|---|---|---|---|
| Jessie | | | | | | | | | | | |
| Victor | | | | | | | | | | | |
| Samantha | | | | | | | | | | | |
| David | | | | | | | | | | | |

    0  1  2  3  4  5  6  7  8  9  10

_____

3. Which friend practices soccer for the most hours each week? _____

## PROBLEM SOLVING  REAL WORLD

4. Which friends practice soccer for fewer than 4 hours each week?

_____

Chapter 10

two hundred thirty-one **P231**

## Lesson Check (CC.2.MD.10)

1. Use the bar graph. How many more children chose summer than spring?

   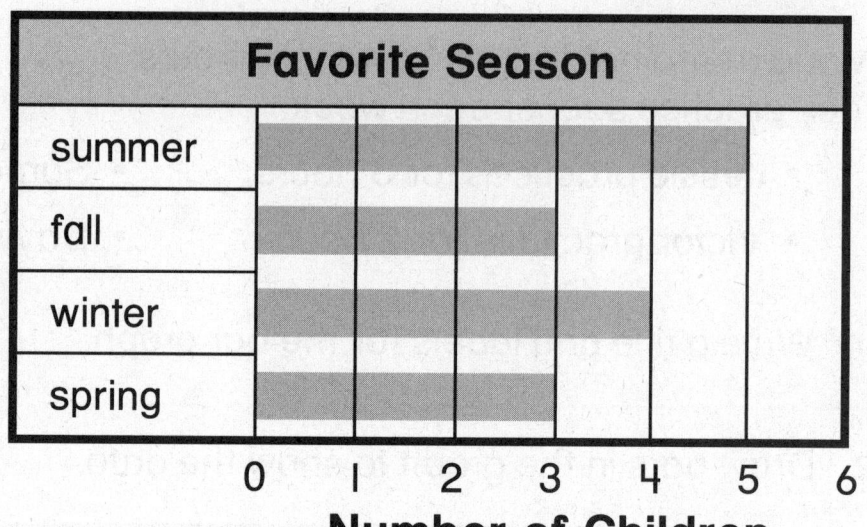

   - ○ 2
   - ○ 3
   - ○ 5
   - ○ 8

## Spiral Review (CC.2.MD.1, CC.2.MD.5, CC.2.MD.6, CC.2.MD.7, CC.2.MD.8)

2. Rachel's chain is 22 centimeters long. She takes 9 centimeters off the chain. How long is Rachel's chain now? (Lesson 9.4)

   - ○ 31 centimeters
   - ○ 29 centimeters
   - ○ 17 centimeters
   - ○ 13 centimeters

3. Use an inch ruler. What is the length of the string to the nearest inch? (Lesson 8.4)

   - ○ 1 inch
   - ○ 2 inches
   - ○ 4 inches
   - ○ 6 inches

4. Gail finished studying at quarter past 1. What time did Gail finish studying? (Lesson 7.10)

   - ○ 1:15
   - ○ 3:50
   - ○ 4:30
   - ○ 5:45

5. Jill has two $1 bills, 1 quarter, and 1 nickel. How much money does Jill have? (Lesson 7.7)

   - ○ $2.35
   - ○ $2.30
   - ○ $2.05
   - ○ $1.30

Name _____

## Problem Solving • Display Data

**Make a bar graph to solve the problem.**

1. The list shows the number of books that Abby read each month. Describe how the number of books she read changed from February to May.

| February | 8 books |
|---|---|
| March | 7 books |
| April | 6 books |
| May | 4 books |

**PROBLEM SOLVING**
**Lesson 10.6**

COMMON CORE STANDARD CC.2.MD.10
Represent and interpret data.

|  |  |  |  |  |  |  |  |  |  |  |
|---|---|---|---|---|---|---|---|---|---|---|
| February |  |  |  |  |  |  |  |  |  |  |
| March |  |  |  |  |  |  |  |  |  |  |
| April |  |  |  |  |  |  |  |  |  |  |
| May |  |  |  |  |  |  |  |  |  |  |

0  1  2  3  4  5  6  7  8  9  10

_____

The number of books _____

_____

2. How many books in all did Abby read in February and March?

_____ books

3. How many fewer books did Abby read in April than in February?

_____ fewer books

4. In which months did Abby read fewer than 7 books?

_____

Chapter 10

two hundred thirty-three  **P233**

# Lesson Check (CC.2.MD.10)

1. Use the bar graph. Which of the following describes how the number of hours changed from Week 1 to Week 4?

   ○ The number of hours decreased.
   ○ The number of hours increased and then decreased.
   ○ The number of hours increased.
   ○ The number of hours stayed the same.

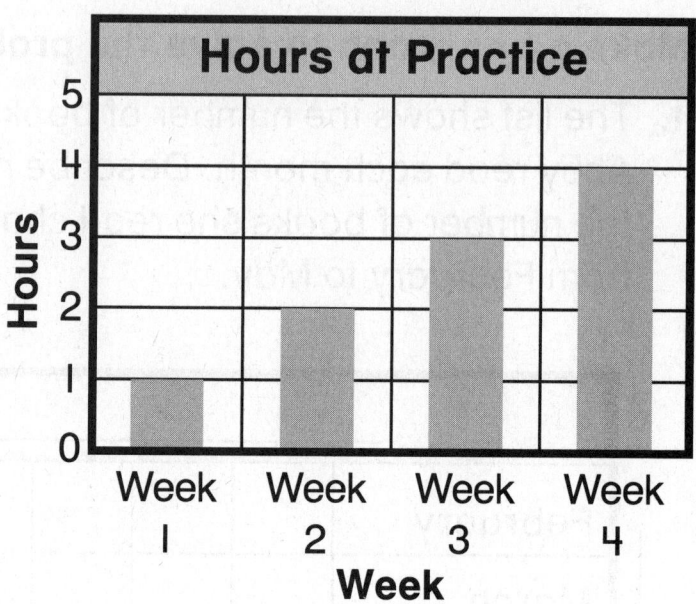

# Spiral Review (CC.2.MD.3, CC.2.MD.8)

2. The string is about 10 centimeters long. Which is the best estimate for the length of the feather? (Lesson 9.2)

   ○ 2 centimeters          ○ 10 centimeters
   ○ 5 centimeters          ○ 20 centimeters

3. What is the total value of this group of coins? (Lesson 7.3)

   ○ 55¢          ○ 40¢
   ○ 50¢          ○ 28¢

4. Rick has one $1 bill, 2 dimes, and 3 pennies. How much money does Rick have? (Lesson 7.6)

   ○ $1.72
   ○ $1.53
   ○ $1.40
   ○ $1.23

Name _____

# Chapter 10 Extra Practice

**Lesson 10.2** (pp. 473–476)

Use the picture graph.

| Favorite Flavor | | | | | |
|---|---|---|---|---|---|
| vanilla | ☺ | ☺ | ☺ | | |
| chocolate | ☺ | ☺ | ☺ | ☺ | |
| strawberry | ☺ | ☺ | ☺ | ☺ | ☺ |
| mint | ☺ | ☺ | | | |

**Key: Each ☺ stands for 1 child.**

1. How many children chose chocolate?  _____ children

2. Which flavor did the most children choose?  _____

3. How many children in all chose a favorite flavor?  _____ children

**Lesson 10.3** (pp. 477–479)

1. Use the tally chart to complete the picture graph.
Draw a ● for each book.

| Number of Books Read | |
|---|---|
| Name | Tally |
| Maya | IIII |
| Gabe | H̶H̶t̶ |
| Tia | III |
| Cathy | I |

| Number of Books Read | | | | | |
|---|---|---|---|---|---|
| Maya | | | | | |
| Gabe | | | | | |
| Tia | | | | | |
| Cathy | | | | | |

**Key: Each ● stands for 1 book.**

2. Who read more than 4 books?  _____

# Lesson 10.4 (pp. 481–484)

Use the bar graph.

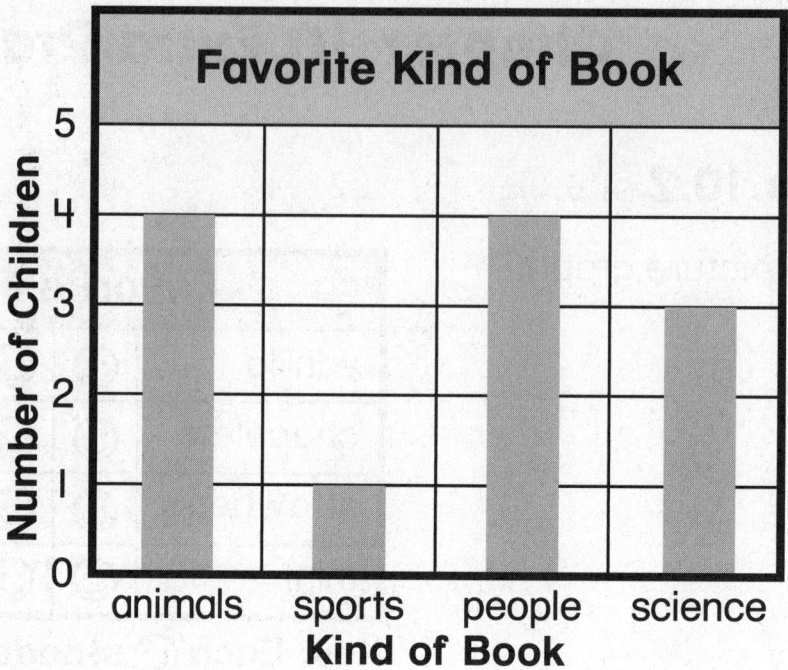

1. Which kind of book did the fewest children choose? _____

2. How many children in all chose a favorite kind of book? _____ children

# Lesson 10.5 (pp. 485–488)

Robin has 5 red beads, 7 blue beads, 8 yellow beads, and 5 green beads.

1. Write a title and labels.
   Draw bars to show the data.

|  | | | | | | | | | |
|---|---|---|---|---|---|---|---|---|---|
| red | | | | | | | | | |
| blue | | | | | | | | | |
| yellow | | | | | | | | | |
| green | | | | | | | | | |

0  1  2  3  4  5  6  7  8  9

# Chapter 11
# School-Home Letter

**Dear Family:**

My class started Chapter 11 this week. In this chapter, I will learn about three-dimensional and two-dimensional shapes. I will also learn about equal parts of a whole.

Love, _____

## Vocabulary

**quadrilateral**

**pentagon**

**hexagon**

**cone**

**cylinder**

**cube**

## Home Activity

Name a two-dimensional shape: triangle, quadrilateral, pentagon, or hexagon. With your child, look for an object that has that shape.

Repeat the activity using a three-dimensional shape: cube, rectangular prism, sphere, cylinder, or cone.

## Literature

Reading math stories reinforces learning. Look for these books at the library.

**Shape Up!** by David Adler. Holiday House, 1998.

**The Village of Round and Square Houses** by Ann Grifalconi. Little, Brown and Company, 1986.

# Capítulo 11
## Carta para la casa

### Querida familia:
Mi clase comenzó hoy el Capítulo 11. En este capítulo, aprenderé acerca de las figuras bidimensionales y tridimensionales. También aprenderé sobre las partes igualdades de un entero.

Con cariño, _____

### Vocabulario

cuadrilátero

pentágono

hexágono

cono

cilindro

cubo

### Actividad para la casa

Nombre alguna figura bidimensional, como triángulo, cuadrilátero, pentágono o hexágono. Juntos, busquen una figura que tenga la misma forma. Repitan la actividad con una figura tridimensional, como cubo, prisma rectangular, esfera, cilindro o cono.

### Literatura

Leer cuentos de matemáticas refuerza el aprendizaje. Busquen estos libros en la biblioteca.

**Shape Up!** por David Adler. Holiday House, 1998

**The Village of Round and Square Houses** por Ann Grifalconi. Little, Brown and Company, 1986.

# Lesson 11.1

Name _____

## Three-Dimensional Shapes

**COMMON CORE STANDARD** CC.2.G.1
Reason with shapes and their attributes.

**Circle the objects that match the shape name.**

| | | | |
|---|---|---|---|
| 1. cube |  |  |  |
| 2. cone |  |  |  |
| 3. rectangular prism |  |  |  |
| 4. cylinder |  |  |  |

## PROBLEM SOLVING

5. Lisa draws a circle by tracing around the bottom of a block. Which could be the shape of Lisa's block? Circle the name of the shape.

     cone          cube          rectangular prism

Chapter 11

## Lesson Check (CC.2.G.1)

1. What is the name of this shape?

   - ○ cube
   - ○ cone
   - ○ cylinder
   - ○ sphere

2. What is the name of this shape?

   - ○ rectangular prism
   - ○ cube
   - ○ sphere
   - ○ cone

## Spiral Review (CC.2.MD.3, CC.2.MD.7, CC.2.MD.8)

3. The string is about 6 centimeters long. Which is the best estimate for the length of the crayon? (Lesson 9.2)

   - ○ 3 centimeters
   - ○ 4 centimeters
   - ○ 9 centimeters
   - ○ 12 centimeters

4. What is the total value of this group of coins? (Lesson 7.1)

   - ○ 3¢
   - ○ 11¢
   - ○ 15¢
   - ○ 16¢

5. What time is shown on this clock? (Lesson 7.8)

   - ○ 6:00
   - ○ 10:06
   - ○ 10:30
   - ○ 11:00

# Lesson 11.2

Name _____

## Attributes of Three-Dimensional Shapes

COMMON CORE STANDARD CC.2.G.1
Reason with shapes and their attributes.

Circle the set of shapes that are the faces of the three-dimensional shape.

1.
rectangular prism

2.
cube

3.
rectangular prism

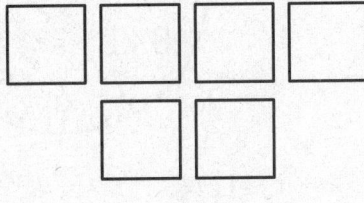

## PROBLEM SOLVING REAL WORLD

4. Kevin keeps his marbles in a container that has the shape of a cube. He wants to paint each face a different color. How many different paint colors does he need?

_____ different paint colors

Chapter 11 two hundred forty-one P241

# Lesson Check (CC.2.G.1)

1. How many faces does a cube have?

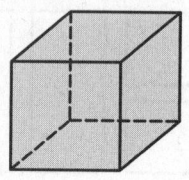

- ○ 8
- ○ 7
- ○ 6
- ○ 5

2. How many faces does a rectangular prism have?

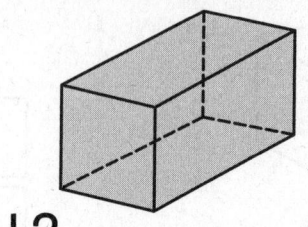

- ○ 12
- ○ 10
- ○ 8
- ○ 6

# Spiral Review (CC.2.MD.7, CC.2.MD.9, CC.2.MD.10, CC.2.G.1)

3. What time is shown on this clock? (Lesson 7.9)

- ○ 9:45
- ○ 9:15
- ○ 9:03
- ○ 3:45

4. Which of these shapes is a cone? (Lesson 11.1)

○    ○

○    ○

5. Use the line plot. How many books are 8 inches long? (Lesson 8.9)

- ○ 1
- ○ 2
- ○ 6
- ○ 8

```
              X
       X      X
       X      X      X      X
       X      X      X      X
    ┼──────┼──────┼──────┼
    5      6      7      8
```

**Lengths of Books in Inches**

Name _____

## Two-Dimensional Shapes

**Lesson 11.3**

**COMMON CORE STANDARD** CC.2.G.1
Reason with shapes and their attributes.

Write the number of sides and the number of vertices. Then write the name of the shape.

pentagon        triangle
hexagon         quadrilateral

1.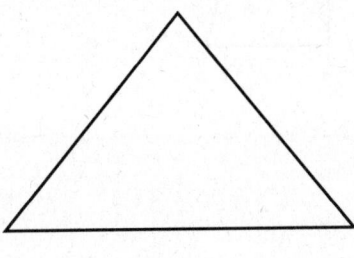
___ sides
___ vertices
_____

2.
___ sides
___ vertices
_____

3.
___ sides
___ vertices
_____

4.
___ sides
___ vertices
_____

5.
___ sides
___ vertices
_____

6.
___ sides
___ vertices
_____

### PROBLEM SOLVING REAL WORLD

Solve. Draw or write to explain.

7. Oscar is drawing a picture of a house. He draws a pentagon shape for a window. How many sides does his window have?

____ sides

Chapter 11

two hundred forty-three **P243**

# Lesson Check (CC.2.G.1)

1. How many sides does a hexagon have?

- ○ 3
- ○ 4
- ○ 5
- ○ 6

2. How many vertices does a quadrilateral have?

- ○ 6
- ○ 5
- ○ 4
- ○ 3

# Spiral Review (CC.2.MD.1, CC.2.MD.10)

3. Use a centimeter ruler. What is the length of the ribbon to the nearest centimeter? (Lesson 9.3)

- ○ 10 centimeters
- ○ 14 centimeters
- ○ 16 centimeters
- ○ 18 centimeters

4. Look at the picture graph. How many more children chose apples than chose oranges? (Lesson 10.3)

- ○ 1
- ○ 2
- ○ 4
- ○ 11

| Favorite Fruit | | | | |
|---|---|---|---|---|
| apples | ☺ | ☺ | ☺ | ☺ |
| oranges | ☺ | ☺ | | |
| grapes | ☺ | ☺ | ☺ | |
| peaches | ☺ | ☺ | | |

Key: Each ☺ stands for 1 child.

Name _____

# Angles in Two-Dimensional Shapes

**Lesson 11.4**

**COMMON CORE STANDARD** CC.2.G.1
Reason with shapes and their attributes.

**Circle the angles in each shape.
Write how many.**

1.

   ____ angles

2.

   ____ angles

3.

   ____ angles

4.

   ____ angles

## PROBLEM SOLVING — REAL WORLD

5. Logan drew 2 two-dimensional shapes that had 8 angles in all. Draw shapes Logan could have drawn.

Chapter 11

two hundred forty-five **P245**

## Lesson Check (CC.2.G.1)

1. How many angles does this shape have?

   ○ 3   ○ 5
   ○ 4   ○ 6

2. How many angles does this shape have?

   ○ 3   ○ 5
   ○ 4   ○ 6

## Spiral Review (CC.2.MD.5, CC.2.MD.6, CC.2.MD.10, CC.2.G.1)

3. Use an inch ruler. What is the length of the string to the nearest inch? (Lesson 8.4)

   ○ 13 inches    ○ 5 inches
   ○ 11 inches    ○ 3 inches

4. Look at the picture graph. How many children chose daisies?

   (Lesson 10.2)

   ○ 2
   ○ 3
   ○ 4
   ○ 5

   | Favorite Flower | | | | | |
   |---|---|---|---|---|---|
   | roses | ☺ | ☺ | ☺ | ☺ | |
   | tulips | ☺ | ☺ | ☺ | | |
   | daisies | ☺ | ☺ | ☺ | ☺ | ☺ |
   | lillies | ☺ | ☺ | | | |

   Key: Each ☺ stands for 1 child.

Name _____

# Sort Two-Dimensional Shapes

**Lesson 11.5**

**COMMON CORE STANDARD CC.2.G.1**
Reason with shapes and their attributes.

**Circle the shapes that match the rule.**

1. Shapes with fewer than 5 sides

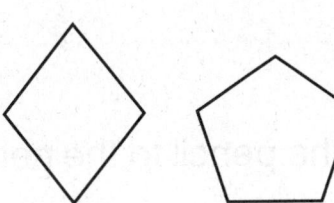

2. Shapes with more than 4 sides

3. Shapes with 4 angles

4. Shapes with fewer than 6 angles

## PROBLEM SOLVING REAL WORLD

Circle the correct shape.

5. Tammy drew a shape with more than 3 angles. It is not a hexagon. Which shape did Tammy draw?

Chapter 11

two hundred forty-seven **P247**

# Lesson Check (CC.2.G.1)

1. Which shape has fewer than 4 sides?

○ ○ ○ ○

# Spiral Review (CC.2.MD.1, CC.2.MD.10)

2. Use an inch ruler. What is the length of the pencil to the nearest inch? (Lesson 8.4)

○ 1 inch
○ 2 inches
○ 6 inches
○ 8 inches

3. Use the tally chart. How many children chose basketball as their favorite sport? (Lesson 10.1)

○ 4
○ 5
○ 6
○ 7

| Favorite Sport ||
| Sport | Tally |
|---|---|
| soccer | ||||| |
| basketball | ||||| || |
| football | |||| |
| baseball | |||| |

# HANDS ON
## Lesson 11.6

Name _____

## Partition Rectangles

**COMMON CORE STANDARD** CC.2.G.2
Reason with shapes and their attributes.

Use color tiles to cover the rectangle.
Trace around the square tiles.
Write how many.

1.

   Number of rows: _____

   Number of columns: _____

   Total: _____ square tiles

2.

   Number of rows: _____

   Number of columns: _____

   Total: _____ square tiles

## PROBLEM SOLVING

Solve. Write or draw to explain.

3. Nina wants to put color tiles on a square. 3 color tiles fit across the top of the square. How many rows and columns of of squares will Nina need? How many color tiles will she use in all?

   Number of rows: _____

   Number of columns: _____

   Total: _____ square tiles

   _____ tiles

Chapter 11

two hundred forty-nine  P249

## Lesson Check (CC.2.G.2)

1. Use color tiles to cover the rectangle. How many tiles did you use?
   - ○ 1
   - ○ 2
   - ○ 3
   - ○ 4

## Spiral Review (CC.2.MD.10, CC.2.G.1)

2. How many faces does a cube have? (Lesson 11.2)

   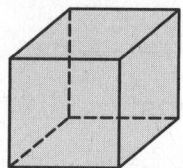

   - ○ 4         ○ 8
   - ○ 6         ○ 10

3. How many angles does this shape have? (Lesson 11.4)

   - ○ 6         ○ 8
   - ○ 7         ○ 10

4. Use the tally chart. How many more children chose art than reading? (Lesson 10.1)
   - ○ 10
   - ○ 8
   - ○ 3
   - ○ 2

| Favorite Subject | |
|---|---|
| Subject | Tally |
| reading | ||||| ||| |
| math | ||||| |||| |
| science | ||||| |
| art | ||||| ||||| |

P250  two hundred fifty

Name _____

# Equal Parts

**Lesson 11.7**

COMMON CORE STANDARD CC.2.G.3
Reason with shapes and their attributes.

Write how many equal parts there are in the whole.
Write halves, thirds, or fourths to name the equal parts.

1.

____ equal parts

_____

2.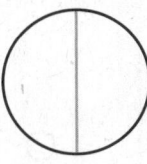

____ equal parts

_____

3.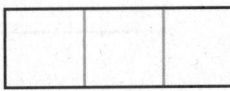

____ equal parts

_____

4.

____ equal parts

_____

5.

____ equal parts

_____

6.

____ equal parts

_____

## PROBLEM SOLVING

7. Sort the shapes.
   - Draw an X on the shapes that do not show equal parts.
   - Circle the shapes that show halves.

Chapter 11     two hundred fifty-one **P251**

# Lesson Check (CC.2.G.3)

1. What are the 3 equal parts of the shape called?

   ○ halves　　○ fourths
   ○ thirds　　○ sixths

2. What are the 4 equal parts of the shape called?

   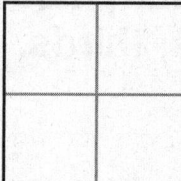

   ○ halves　　○ fourths
   ○ thirds　　○ sixths

# Spiral Review (CC.2.NBT.5, CC.2.G.1)

3. What is the sum? (Lesson 4.7)

   $$\begin{array}{r}87\\+45\\\hline\end{array}$$

   ○ 132　　○ 122
   ○ 112　　○ 42

4. What is the difference? (Lesson 5.2)

   $$\begin{array}{r}59\\-15\\\hline\end{array}$$

   ○ 24　　○ 34
   ○ 44　　○ 74

5. Which of the following shapes is a quadrilateral? (Lesson 11.3)

   ○ 　　○
   ○ 　　○

6. Which of the following shapes is a hexagon? (Lesson 11.3)

   ○ 　　○
   ○ 　　○

Name _____

# Show Equal Parts of a Whole

**Lesson 11.8**

COMMON CORE STANDARD CC.2.G.3
Reason with shapes and their attributes.

**Draw to show equal parts.**

1. halves

2. fourths

3. thirds

4. thirds

5. halves

6. fourths

7. fourths

8. halves

9. thirds

**PROBLEM SOLVING**

Solve. Write or draw to explain.

10. Joe has one sandwich. He cuts the sandwich into fourths. How many pieces of sandwich does he have?

_____ pieces

Chapter 11

two hundred fifty-three **P253**

# Lesson Check (CC.2.G.3)

1. Which shape is divided into fourths?

○ ○ ○ ○

# Spiral Review (CC.2.MD.4, CC.2.G.1)

2. How many angles does this shape have? (Lesson 11.4)

○ 5   ○ 7
○ 6   ○ 8

3. How many faces does a rectangular prism have? (Lesson 11.2)

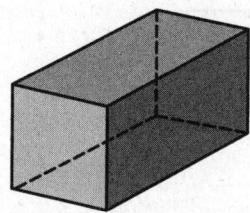

○ 4   ○ 8
○ 6   ○ 12

4. Use a centimeter ruler. Measure the length of each object. How much longer is the ribbon than the string? (Lesson 9.7)

○  2 centimeters longer
○  3 centimeters longer
○  5 centimeters longer
○  17 centimeters longer

Name _____

**Describe Equal Parts**

**Lesson 11.9**

COMMON CORE STANDARD CC.2.G.3
Reason with shapes and their attributes.

Draw to show halves.
Color a half of the shape.

1.

2.

Draw to show thirds.
Color a third of the shape.

3.

4.

Draw to show fourths.
Color a fourth of the shape.

5.

6.

## PROBLEM SOLVING

7. Circle all the shapes that have a third of the shape shaded.

    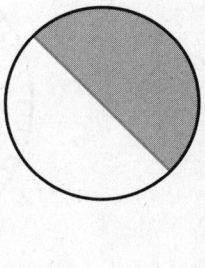

Chapter 11

two hundred fifty-five **P255**

# Lesson Check (CC.2.G.3)

1. Which of these has a half of the shape shaded?

   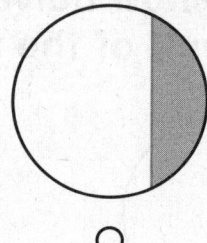

○ ○ ○ ○

# Spiral Review (CC.2.MD.1, CC.2.MD.7, CC.2.G.1)

2. What is the name of this shape?
   (Lesson 11.2)

   ○ hexagon
   ○ pentagon
   ○ rectangle
   ○ triangle

3. Use a centimeter ruler. What is the length of the string to the nearest centimeter? (Lesson 9.3)

   ○ 2 centimeters
   ○ 4 centimeters
   ○ 6 centimeters
   ○ 8 centimeters

4. The clock shows the time Chris finished his homework. What time did Chris finish his homework? (Lesson 7.11)

   ○ 2:10 A.M.   ○ 6:10 P.M.
   ○ 2:30 A.M.   ○ 2:30 P.M.

5. What time is shown on this clock? (Lesson 7.9)

   ○ 3:40   ○ 8:15
   ○ 8:03   ○ 9:15

P256 two hundred fifty-six

Name _____

# Problem Solving • Equal Shares

**PROBLEM SOLVING**
**Lesson 11.10**

COMMON CORE STANDARD CC.2.G.3
Reason with shapes and their attributes.

**Draw to show your answer.**

1. Max has square pizzas that are the same size. What are two different ways he can divide the pizzas into fourths?

2. Lia has two pieces of paper that are the same size. What are two different ways she can divide the pieces of paper into halves?

3. Frank has two crackers that are the same size. What are two different ways he can divide the cracker into thirds?

Chapter 11

two hundred fifty-seven **P257**

# Lesson Check (CC.2.G.3)

1. Bree cut a piece of cardboard into thirds like this.

   Which of these shows another way to cut the cardboard into thirds?

   ○     ○     ○     ○

# Spiral Review (CC.2.MD.7, CC.2.MD.8, CC.2.G.1)

2. Which shape has 3 equal parts? (Lesson 11.7)

3. How many angles does this shape have? (Lesson 11.5)

   ○ 3
   ○ 4
   ○ 5
   ○ 6

   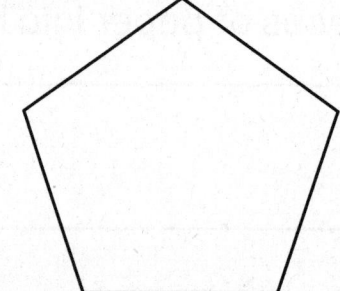

4. What is the best estimate for the width of a door? (Lesson 10.4)

   ○ 1 foot
   ○ 3 feet
   ○ 6 feet
   ○ 10 feet

5. Which is another way to write 10 minutes after 9? (Lesson 7.10)

   ○ 8:50
   ○ 9:10
   ○ 9:50
   ○ 10:10

Name _____

COMMON CORE STANDARDS CC.2.G.1, CC.2.G.2, CC.2.G.3

# Chapter 11 Extra Practice

## Lessons 11.1–11.2 (pp. 509–516)
Circle the objects that match the shape name.

1. rectangular prism

Circle the set of shapes that are the faces of the three-dimensional shape.

2.

## Lesson 11.3 (pp. 517–520)
Write the number of sides and the number of vertices.

1.
\_\_\_ sides
\_\_\_ vertices

2.
\_\_\_ sides
\_\_\_ vertices

3.
\_\_\_ sides
\_\_\_ vertices

# Lesson 11.4 (pp. 521–524)
Circle the angles in each shape. Write how many.

1.

____ angles

2.

____ angles

# Lesson 11.5 (pp. 525–528)
Circle the shapes that match the rule.

1. Shapes with fewer than 4 sides

2. Shapes with 5 angles

# Lesson 11.7 (pp. 533–536)
Write how many equal parts there are in the whole.
Write halves, thirds, or fourths to name the equal parts.

1.

____ equal parts

_____

2.

____ equal parts

_____

3.

____ equal parts

_____

# Lesson 11.8 (pp. 537–540)
Draw to show equal parts.

1. fourths

2. halves

P260  two hundred sixty

# Lesson 1

**Name** _____

## Find Sums on an Addition Table

**Essential Question** How do you find sums on an addition table?

### Model and Draw

$3 + 4 = ?$

The sum for $3 + 4$ is found where row 3 and column 4 meet.

$3 + 4 = \underline{\ 7\ }$

| + | 0 | 1 | 2 | 3 | ④ |
|---|---|---|---|---|---|
| 0 | 0 | 1 | 2 | 3 | 4 |
| 1 | 1 | 2 | 3 | 4 | 5 |
| 2 | 2 | 3 | 4 | 5 | 6 |
| ③ | 3 | 4 | 5 | 6 | ⑦ |
| 4 | 4 | 5 | 6 | 7 | 8 |

## Share and Show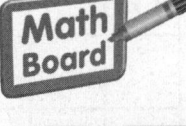

1. Write the missing sums in the addition table.

| + | 0 | 1 | 2 | 3 | 4 | 5 | 6 | 7 | 8 | 9 | 10 |
|---|---|---|---|---|---|---|---|---|---|---|----|
| 0 | 0 | 1 | 2 | 3 | 4 | 5 | 6 |   |   | 9 |    |
| 1 | 1 | 2 | 3 | 4 | 5 | 6 |   |   | 9 |   | 11 |
| 2 | 2 | 3 | 4 | 5 | 6 |   |   | 9 |   | 11 | 12 |
| 3 | 3 | 4 | 5 | 6 |   |   | 9 |   | 11 | 12 | 13 |
| 4 | 4 | 5 | 6 |   |   | 9 |   | 11 | 12 | 13 | 14 |
| 5 | 5 | 6 |   |   | 9 |   | 11 | 12 | 13 | 14 | 15 |
| 6 | 6 |   |   | 9 |   | 11 | 12 | 13 | 14 | 15 | 16 |
| 7 |   |   | 9 |   | 11 | 12 | 13 | 14 | 15 | 16 | 17 |
| 8 |   | 9 |   | 11 | 12 | 13 | 14 | 15 | 16 | 17 | 18 |
| 9 | 9 |   | 11 | 12 | 13 | 14 | 15 | 16 | 17 | 18 | 19 |
| 10 |   | 11 | 12 | 13 | 14 | 15 | 16 | 17 | 18 | 19 | 20 |

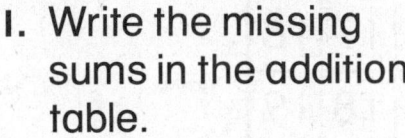

**Math Talk**  Describe a pattern in the addition table.

Getting Ready for Grade 3

# On Your Own

**2.** Write the missing sums in the addition table.

| + | 0 | 1 | 2 | 3 | 4 | 5 | 6 | 7 | 8 | 9 | 10 |
|---|---|---|---|---|---|---|---|---|---|---|----|
| 0 | 0 | 1 | 2 | 3 | 4 | 5 | 6 | 7 | 8 | 9 | 10 |
| 1 | 1 | 2 |   | 4 | 5 | 6 | 7 | 8 | 9 | 10 |   |
| 2 | 2 | 3 | 4 | 5 | 6 | 7 | 8 | 9 | 10 |   | 12 |
| 3 | 3 | 4 | 5 | 6 | 7 | 8 | 9 | 10 |   | 12 |   |
| 4 | 4 | 5 | 6 | 7 | 8 | 9 | 10 |   | 12 |   |   |
| 5 | 5 | 6 | 7 | 8 | 9 | 10 |   | 12 |   |   | 15 |
| 6 | 6 | 7 | 8 | 9 | 10 |   | 12 |   |   | 15 | 16 |
| 7 | 7 | 8 | 9 | 10 |   | 12 |   |   | 15 | 16 | 17 |
| 8 | 8 | 9 | 10 |   | 12 |   |   | 15 | 16 | 17 | 18 |
| 9 | 9 | 10 |   | 12 |   |   | 15 | 16 | 17 | 18 | 19 |
| 10 | 10 |   | 12 |   |   | 15 | 16 | 17 | 18 | 19 | 20 |

# PROBLEM SOLVING  REAL WORLD

Solve. Write or draw to explain.

**3.** Natasha has 13 apples. Some apples are red and some are green. She has more red apples than green apples. How many red apples and how many green apples could she have?

**TAKE HOME ACTIVITY** • Ask your child to explain how to use the addition table to find the sum of 8 + 6.

Name _____

**Lesson 2**

# Estimate Sums: 2-Digit Addition

**Essential Question** How can you estimate the sum of two 2-digit numbers?

## Model and Draw

Estimate the sum of 24 + 38.
Find the nearest ten for each number.

__20__ + __40__ = __60__

An estimate of the sum is __60__.

## Share and Show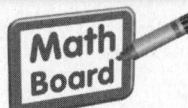

Find the nearest ten for each number.

1. Estimate the sum of 18 + 29.

Add the tens to estimate.

_____ + _____ = _____

An estimate of the sum is _____.

**Math Talk** How did you know which ten is nearest to 18?

Getting Ready for Grade 3

## On Your Own

Find the nearest ten for each number.
Add the tens to estimate.

2. Estimate the sum of 13 + 28.

_____ + _____ = _____

An estimate of the sum is _____.

3. Estimate the sum of 31 + 22.

_____ + _____ = _____

An estimate of the sum is _____.

## PROBLEM SOLVING REAL WORLD

Solve. Write or draw to explain.

4. Mark has 34 pennies. Emma has 47 pennies. About how many pennies do they have altogether?

about _____ pennies

**TAKE HOME ACTIVITY** • Ask your child to use the number line for Exercise 2 and describe how to estimate the sum of 27 + 21.

P264 two hundred sixty-four

Name _____

Lesson 3

# Estimate Sums: 3-Digit Addition

**Essential Question** How can you estimate the sum of two 3-digit numbers?

## Model and Draw

Estimate the sum of 189 + 284.
Find the nearest hundred for each number.

__200__ + __300__ = __500__

An estimate of the sum is __500__.

## Share and Show

Find the nearest hundred for each number.
Add the hundreds to estimate.

1. Estimate the sum of 229 + 386.

_____ + _____ = _____

An estimate of the sum is _____.

**Math Talk** How do you know which two hundreds a 3-digit number is between?

Getting Ready for Grade 3

two hundred sixty-five **P265**

## On Your Own

Find the nearest hundred for each number.
Add the hundreds to estimate.

2. Estimate the sum of 324 + 218.

_____ + _____ = _____

An estimate of the sum is _____.

3. Estimate the sum of 468 + 439.

_____ + _____ = _____

An estimate of the sum is _____.

## PROBLEM SOLVING REAL WORLD

Solve. Write or draw to explain.

4. There are 375 yellow fish and 283 blue fish swimming around a coral reef. About how many fish are there altogether?

about _____ fish

**TAKE HOME ACTIVITY** • Ask your child to use the number line for Exercise 2 and describe how to estimate the sum of 215 + 398.

Name _____

**Lesson 4**

# Estimate Differences: 2-Digit Subtraction

**Essential Question** How can you estimate the difference of two 2-digit numbers?

## Model and Draw

Estimate the difference of 62 − 48.
Find the nearest ten for each number.

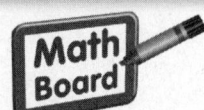

__60__ − __50__ = __10__

An estimate of the difference is __10__.

## Share and Show

Find the nearest ten for each number.
Subtract the tens to estimate.

1. Estimate the difference of 42 − 29.

_____ − _____ = _____

An estimate of the difference is _____.

**Math Talk** How do you know which two tens a number is between?

**Getting Ready for Grade 3** two hundred sixty-seven **P267**

## On Your Own

Find the nearest ten for each number.
Subtract the tens to estimate.

2. Estimate the difference of 51 − 39.

_____ − _____ = _____

An estimate of the difference is _____.

3. Estimate the difference of 79 − 56.

_____ − _____ = _____

An estimate of the difference is _____.

## PROBLEM SOLVING REAL WORLD

Solve. Write or draw to explain.

4. A farmer has 91 cows. 58 of the cows are in the barn. About how many of the cows are not in the barn?

about _____ cows

**TAKE HOME ACTIVITY** • Ask your child to use the number line for Exercise 2 and describe how to estimate the difference of 57 − 41.

Name _____

**Lesson 5**

# Estimate Differences: 3-Digit Subtraction

**Essential Question** How can you estimate the difference of two 3-digit numbers?

### Model and Draw

Estimate the difference of 382 − 265.
Find the nearest hundred for each number.

__400__ − __300__ = __100__

An estimate of the difference is __100__.

## Share and Show

Find the nearest hundred for each number.
Subtract the hundreds to estimate.

1. Estimate the difference of 674 − 590.

_____ − _____ = _____

An estimate of the difference is _____.

**Math Talk**  How did you know which hundred is nearest to 674?

Getting Ready for Grade 3 — two hundred sixty-nine **P269**

## On Your Own

Find the nearest hundred for each number.
Subtract the hundreds to estimate.

2. Estimate the difference of 791 − 612.

_____ − _____ = _____

An estimate of the difference is _____.

3. Estimate the difference of 487 − 309.

_____ − _____ = _____

An estimate of the difference is _____.

## PROBLEM SOLVING REAL WORLD

Solve. Write or draw to explain.

4. A mail carrier had 819 letters to deliver. Then she delivered 687 letters. About how many letters does she still have to deliver?

about _____ letters

**TAKE HOME ACTIVITY** • Ask your child to use the number line for Exercise 2 and describe how to estimate the difference of 786 − 611.

Name _____

**Lesson 6**

# Order 3-Digit Numbers

**Essential Question:** How does place value help you order 3-digit numbers?

## Model and Draw

You can order 249, 418, and 205 from least to greatest. First, compare the **hundreds**. Next, compare the tens and then the ones, if needed.

| Hundreds | Tens | Ones |
|----------|------|------|
| 2 | 4 | 9 |
| 4 | 1 | 8 |
| 2 | 0 | 5 |

*I compare the hundreds. 249 and 205 are both less than 418.*

*Which is less, 249 or 205? I compare the tens. 205 is less than 249, so 205 is the least.*

$\underline{205}$ < $\underline{249}$ < $\underline{418}$
least              greatest

## Share and Show

Write the numbers in order from least to greatest.

1.  
672  
515  
532  

___ < ___ < ___

2.  
787  
683  
564  

___ < ___ < ___

 **Math Talk** Do you always need to compare the ones digits when you order numbers? Explain.

Getting Ready for Grade 3      two hundred seventy-one **P271**

## On Your Own

Write the numbers in order from least to greatest.

3.
359
715
608

____ < ____ < ____

4.
959
915
908

____ < ____ < ____

5.
343
341
348

____ < ____ < ____

6.
165
746
764

____ < ____ < ____

## PROBLEM SOLVING REAL WORLD

7. Brenda, Jean, and Pam play a video game. Brenda scores the highest. Jean scores the lowest.

| Brenda | 863 |
|--------|-----|
| Jean   | 767 |
| Pam    | ?   |

On the line, write a 3-digit number that could be Pam's score.

767 < ____ < 863

**TAKE HOME ACTIVITY** • Write three 3-digit numbers. Have your child tell you how to order the numbers from least to greatest.

Name _____

## ✓ Checkpoint

**Concepts and Skills**

1. Write the missing sums in the addition table.

| + | 0 | 1 | 2 | 3 | 4 | 5 | 6 | 7 | 8 | 9 | 10 |
|---|---|---|---|---|---|---|---|---|---|---|----|
| 0 | 0 | 1 | 2 | 3 | 4 | 5 |   | 7 |   | 9 |    |
| 1 | 1 | 2 | 3 | 4 | 5 |   | 7 |   | 9 |   | 11 |
| 2 | 2 | 3 | 4 | 5 |   | 7 |   | 9 |   | 11 | 12 |
| 3 | 3 | 4 | 5 |   | 7 |   | 9 |   | 11 | 12 | 13 |
| 4 | 4 | 5 |   | 7 |   | 9 |   | 11 | 12 | 13 | 14 |
| 5 | 5 |   | 7 |   | 9 |   | 11 | 12 | 13 | 14 | 15 |

Find the nearest ten.

2. Estimate the sum of 24 and 36.

_____ + _____ = _____

An estimate of the sum is _____.

Find the nearest hundred.

3. Estimate the sum of 285 and 122.

_____ + _____ = _____

An estimate of the sum is _____.

Getting Ready for Grade 3      two hundred seventy-three   **P273**

Find the nearest ten.

4. Estimate the difference of 72 − 59.

_____ − _____ = _____

An estimate of the difference is _____.

---

Find the nearest hundred.

5. Estimate the difference of 792 and 619.

_____ − _____ = _____

An estimate of the difference is _____.

---

6. Which of the following numbers will make this true?

350 < 413 < _____.

○ 403

○ 398

○ 430

○ 331

Name _____

**Lesson 7**

## Equal Groups of 2

**Essential Question:** How can you find the total number in equal groups of 2?

### Model and Draw

The pet store has 3 fishbowls in the window. There are 2 goldfish in each bowl. How many goldfish are there in all?

*I can count the equal groups by twos—2, 4, 6—to find how many in all.*

Make 3 groups of 2 counters.

___3___ groups of ___2___ is ___6___ in all.

## Share and Show

Complete the sentence to show how many in all.

1.

   _____ groups of _____ is _____ in all.

2.

   _____ groups of _____ is _____ in all.

3.

   _____ groups of _____ is _____ in all.

 **Math Talk** How can you use counters to find 2 + 2 + 2 + 2 + 2?

**Getting Ready for Grade 3**

# On Your Own

Complete the sentence to show how many in all.

4.

   _____ groups of _____ is _____ in all.

5.

   _____ groups of _____ is _____ in all.

6.

   _____ groups of _____ is _____ in all.

7.

   _____ groups of _____ is _____ in all.

# PROBLEM SOLVING REAL WORLD

Solve. Write or draw to explain.

8. Coach Baker keeps 2 basketballs in each bin. There are 5 bins. How many basketballs are stored in the bins?

   _____ basketballs

 **TAKE HOME ACTIVITY** • Have your child draw groups of two Xs and tell you how to find how many there are in all.

Name _____

**Lesson 8**

## Equal Groups of 5

**Essential Question:** How can you find the total number in equal groups of 5?

### Model and Draw

Luke made 3 cube trains. He connected 5 cubes in each train. How many cubes did he use in all?

Make 3 groups of 5 cubes.

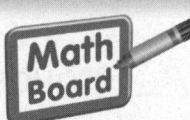

I can count the equal groups by fives—5, 10, 15—to find how many in all.

__3__ groups of __5__ is __15__ in all.

## Share and Show

Complete the sentence to show how many in all.

1.

   ____ groups of ____ is ____ in all.

2.

   ____ groups of ____ is ____ in all.

3.

   ____ groups of ____ is ____ in all.

**Math Talk** How can you use addition to find how many in all in Exercise 2?

**Getting Ready for Grade 3**

two hundred seventy-seven **P277**

## On Your Own

Complete the sentences to show how many in all.

4.  ____ groups of ____ is ____ in all.

5.  ____ groups of ____ is ____ in all.

6.  ____ groups of ____ is ____ in all.

## PROBLEM SOLVING REAL WORLD

Solve. Write or draw to explain.

7. Gina fills 6 pages of her photo album. She puts 5 photos on each page. How many photos does Gina put in her album?

____ photos

**TAKE HOME ACTIVITY** • Place your hands next to your child's hands. Ask how many groups of 5 fingers. Have your child tell you how to find how many in all. How many fingers in all?

Name _____

Lesson 9

## Equal Groups of 10

**Essential Question:** How can you find the total number in equal groups of 10?

### Model and Draw

There are 4 packs of juice. Each pack has 10 juice boxes. How many juice boxes are there in all?

Make 4 groups of 10 cubes.

I can count the equal groups by tens—10, 20, 30, 40—to find how many in all.

__4__ groups of __10__ is __40__ in all.

### Share and Show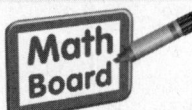

Complete the sentence to show how many in all.

1.

____ groups of ____ is ____ in all.

2.

____ groups of ____ is ____ in all.

3.

____ groups of ____ is ____ in all.

 **Math Talk** How many groups of ten are in 70? Explain.

Getting Ready for Grade 3

two hundred seventy-nine **P279**

## On Your Own

Complete the sentence to show how many in all.

4.

_____ groups of _____ is _____ in all.

5.

_____ groups of _____ is _____ in all.

6.

_____ groups of _____ is _____ in all.

## PROBLEM SOLVING REAL WORLD

Solve. Write or draw to explain.

7. To count his pennies, Travis puts 10 pennies in a stack. He makes 4 stacks. How many pennies does Travis have?

_____ pennies

**TAKE HOME ACTIVITY** • Give your child 30 pieces of macaroni or other small objects. Have your child make groups of 10. Ask how many groups there are. Ask your child to tell you how to find how many in all. How many pieces in all?

Name _____

**HANDS ON
Lesson 10**

## Size of Shares

**Essential Question** How can you place items in equal groups?

### Model and Draw

When you divide, you place items in equal groups.

Joel has 12 carrots. There are 6 rabbits. Each rabbit gets the same number of carrots. How many carrots does each rabbit get?

Place 12 counters in 6 equal groups.

__2__ counters in each group     So, each rabbit gets __2__ carrots.

### Share and Show

Use counters. Draw to show your work.
Write how many in each group.

1. Place 10 counters in 2 equal groups.

_____ counters in each group

2. Place 6 counters in 3 equal groups.

_____ counters in each group

**Math Talk** How did you know how many counters to place in each group for Exercise 2?

Getting Ready for Grade 3

# On Your Own

Use counters. Draw to show your work.
Write how many in each group.

3. Place 9 counters in 3 equal groups.

   _____ counters in each group

4. Place 12 counters in 2 equal groups.

   _____ counters in each group

5. Place 16 counters in 4 equal groups.

   _____ counters in each group

# PROBLEM SOLVING  REAL WORLD

Solve. Draw to show your work.

6. Mrs. Peters divides 6 orange slices between 2 plates. She wants to have 4 orange slices on each plate. How many more orange slices does she need?

   _____ more orange slices

**TAKE HOME ACTIVITY** • Ask your child to place 15 pennies into 3 equal groups, and then tell how many pennies are in each group.

Name _____

**HANDS ON
Lesson 11**

# Number of Equal Shares

**Essential Question** How can you find the number of equal groups that items can be placed into?

## Model and Draw

There are 12 cookies. 3 cookies fill a snack bag. How many snack bags can be filled?

Place 12 counters in groups of 3.

      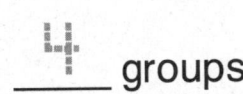 groups

So, __4__ snack bags can be filled.

## Share and Show

Use counters. Draw to show your work.
Write how many groups.

1. Place 8 counters in groups of 4.

_____ groups

2. Place 10 counters in groups of 2.

_____ groups

 **Math Talk** Describe how you could find the number of groups of 2 you could make with 12 counters.

Getting Ready for Grade 3

# On Your Own

Use counters. Draw to show your work.
Write how many groups.

3. Place 4 counters in groups of 2.

_____ groups

4. Place 12 counters in groups of 4.

_____ groups

5. Place 15 counters in groups of 3.

_____ groups

# PROBLEM SOLVING

Draw to show your work.

6. Some children want to play a board game. There are 16 game pieces. Each player needs to have 4 pieces. How many children can play?

_____ children

**TAKE HOME ACTIVITY** • Use small items such as pennies or cereal. Have your child find out how many groups of 5 are in 20.

Name _____

# Lesson 12

## Solve Problems with Equal Shares

**Essential Question:** How can you solve word problems that involve equal shares?

### Model and Draw

You can draw a picture to help you solve problems with equal shares.

There are 10 marbles in each bag. How many marbles are in 3 bags?

__3__ groups of __10__ is __30__ in all.

There are __30__ marbles.

## Share and Show

Solve. Draw or write to show what you did.

1. There are 5 oranges in each sack. How many oranges are in 4 sacks?

   _____ oranges

2. Sandy can plant 2 seeds in a pot. How many pots will Sandy need in order to plant 6 seeds?

   _____ pots

 **Math Talk** Explain how you solved Exercise 2.

**Getting Ready for Grade 3**

two hundred eighty-five **P285**

# On Your Own

Solve. Draw to show what you did.

3. Ben gives each friend 2 crackers. How many crackers does he need for 6 friends?

_____ crackers

4. Mrs. Green can pack 5 books in a box. How many boxes will she need in order to pack 15 books?

_____ boxes

# PROBLEM SOLVING

5. Franco used 12 connecting cubes to build towers. All the towers are the same height. Draw a picture to show the towers he could have built.

**TAKE HOME ACTIVITY** • Ask your child to make up a word problem about 3 boxes of toys with 3 toys in each box. Have your child tell you how to solve the problem.

Name _____

# ✓ Checkpoint

## Concepts and Skills

Complete the sentence to show how many in all.

1. ○○ ○○ ○○ ○○ ○○ ○○ ○○

   \_\_\_\_ groups of \_\_\_\_ is \_\_\_\_ in all.

2. 

   \_\_\_\_ groups of \_\_\_\_ is \_\_\_\_ in all.

3.

   \_\_\_\_ groups of \_\_\_\_ is \_\_\_\_ in all.

Getting Ready for Grade 3     two hundred eighty-seven **P287**

Use counters. Draw to show your work.
Write how many in each group.

4. Place 14 counters in 2 equal groups.

_____ counters in each group

---

Use counters. Draw to show your work.
Write how many groups.

5. Place 12 counters in groups of 2.

_____ groups

---

Solve the problem.

6. Mrs. Owen puts 3 flowers in each vase.
   How many flowers are in 4 vases?

   ○ 7

   ○ 9

   ○ 12

   ○ 16

Name _____

# Lesson 13

## Hour Before and Hour After

**Essential Question:** How do you tell the time 1 hour before and 1 hour after a given time?

### Model and Draw

For these times, the minute hand points to the same place. The hour hands point to different numbers.

The time is __8:00__.

The hour hand points to 8.

1 hour before

__7:00__

The hour hand points to 7.

1 hour after

__9:00__

The hour hand points to 9.

## Share and Show

Write the time shown on the clock. Then write the time 1 hour before and 1 hour after.

1.

_____ 1 hour before

_____ 1 hour after

2.

_____ 1 hour before

_____ 1 hour after

 **Math Talk** How are the hands on a clock that shows 8 o'clock the same as the hands on a clock 1 hour after? How are they different?

Getting Ready for Grade 3

two hundred eighty-nine  **P289**

# On Your Own

Write the time shown. Then write the time 1 hour before and 1 hour after.

3.

_____ 1 hour before

_____ 1 hour after

4.

_____ 1 hour before

_____ 1 hour after

5.

_____ 1 hour before

_____ 1 hour after

6.

_____ 1 hour before

_____ 1 hour after

## PROBLEM SOLVING REAL WORLD

7. Tim feeds the cat 1 hour after 7:00. Draw the hour hand and the minute hand to show 1 hour after 7:00. Then write the time.

Tim needs to feed the cat at _____.

**TAKE HOME ACTIVITY** • Ask your child what the time will be 1 hour after 3:30. What time was it 1 hour before 3:30? Have your child tell you how he or she knows.

P290 two hundred ninety

**Lesson 14**

Name _____

# Elapsed Time in Hours

**Essential Question** How do you find the number of hours between two times?

### Model and Draw

Baseball practice starts at 2:00. Everyone leaves practice at 4:00. How long does baseball practice last?
Use the time line to count how many hours passed from 2:00 P.M. to 4:00 P.M.

Starts at 2:00     Ends at 4:00

____ hours

9:00 A.M.   11:00 A.M.   1:00 P.M.   3:00 P.M.   5:00 P.M.
   10:00 A.M.   Noon   2:00 P.M.   4:00 P.M.   6:00 P.M.

## Share and Show

Use the time line above. Solve.

1. The game starts at 3:00 P.M. It ends at 6:00 P.M. How long does the game last?

   ____ hours

2. The plane leaves at 10:00 A.M. It arrives at 2:00 P.M. How long is the plane trip?

   ____ hours

3. Max goes out at 2:00 P.M. He comes back in at 5:00 P.M. For how long was Max out?

   ____ hours

4. Art class starts at 9:00 A.M. It ends at 11:00 A.M. How long is the art class?

   ____ hours

 **Math Talk**  Describe how you used the time line for Exercise 2.

**Getting Ready for Grade 3**                    two hundred ninety-one **P291**

# On Your Own

Use the time line below. Solve.

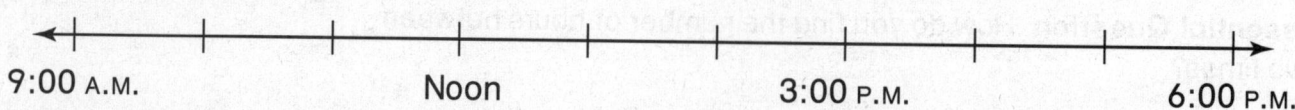

5. Paul's baby sister goes to sleep at 4:00 P.M. She wakes up at 6:00 P.M. How long does the baby sleep?

_____ hours

6. Julia goes to a friend's house at noon. She comes home at 3:00 P.M. How long is Julia gone?

_____ hours

7. Jeff starts raking leaves at 11:00 A.M. He stops at 1:00 P.M. How long does Jeff rake leaves?

_____ hours

8. Mom and Carrie arrive at the shopping mall at 1:00 P.M. They leave at 5:00 P.M. How long are they at the mall?

_____ hours

## PROBLEM SOLVING REAL WORLD

Solve. Draw or write to explain.

9. Mr. Norton writes the time for classes on the board.

| Class | Time |
|---|---|
| Math | 8:30 A.M. |
| Reading | 9:30 A.M. |
| Music | 11:30 A.M. |

How long will reading class last?

_____ hours

**TAKE HOME ACTIVITY** • Ask your child how much time passes between 4:30 and 7:30. Have your child explain how he or she arrived at the answer.

P292 two hundred ninety-two

# Lesson 15

Name _____

## Elapsed Time in Minutes

**Essential Question** How do you find the number of minutes between two times?

### Model and Draw

You can use subtraction if the times are within the same hour.

Ken starts cleaning his room at 3:15 P.M. He finishes at 3:35 P.M. How long does it take Ken to clean his room?

$$\begin{array}{r} 35 \\ -15 \\ \hline 20 \end{array}$$

**Starts at 3:15 P.M.    Ends at 3:35 P.M.**

So it takes Ken __20__ minutes.

## Share and Show

Subtract to solve. Show your work.

1. Leah starts eating lunch at 12:10 P.M. She finishes at 12:25 P.M. How long does it take for Leah to eat lunch?

   ____ minutes

2. Kwan gets on the school bus at 8:10 A.M. He gets to school at 8:55 A.M. How long is Kwan's bus ride?

   ____ minutes

3. Carla takes her dog to the park at 2:05 P.M. She gets back at 2:40 P.M. How long does Carla walk her dog?

   ____ minutes

4. Ethan starts his spelling homework at 6:25 P.M. He finishes at 6:45 P.M. How long does Ethan work on his spelling?

   ____ minutes

**Math Talk** How could you check your answers by looking at a clock?

Getting Ready for Grade 3

# On Your Own

**Subtract to solve. Show your work.**

5. Mrs. Hall puts a pizza in the oven at 6:10 P.M. She takes it out at 6:30 P.M. How long does the pizza bake?

   _____

   _____ minutes

6. The reading test starts at 1:10 P.M. Everyone must stop at 1:25 P.M. How long do the children have to take their test?

   _____ minutes

7. Kelly starts drawing at 8:15 P.M. She finishes her picture at 8:40 P.M. How long does Kelly draw?

   _____

   _____ minutes

8. Tony starts reading at 4:30 P.M. He stops reading at 4:45 P.M. How long does Tony read?

   _____

   _____ minutes

# PROBLEM SOLVING REAL WORLD

Show how to use subtraction to solve.

9. Mr. West gets to the bus stop at 9:05 A.M. He looks at the bus schedule.

   | Bus Arrival Times |
   |---|
   | 8:30 A.M. |
   | 9:30 A.M. |
   | 10:30 A.M. |

   How long will Mr. West need to wait for a bus?

   _____ minutes

**TAKE HOME ACTIVITY** • Have your child track how many minutes it would take to do math homework if he or she starts at 5:15 P.M. and stops at 5:45 P.M.

P294 two hundred ninety-four

Name _____

**HANDS ON Lesson 16**

# Capacity • Nonstandard Units

**Essential Question** How can you measure how much a container holds?

## Model and Draw

Use a scoop and rice to estimate and measure how much a can holds.

- Estimate how many scoops the can holds.
- Fill a scoop with rice or water.
- Pour it into the can.
- Repeat until the can is full. Keep track of the number of scoops.

## Share and Show

How many scoops does the container hold? Estimate. Then measure.

| Container | Estimate | Measure |
|---|---|---|
| 1. mug | about ____ scoops | about ____ scoops |
| 2. vase | about ____ scoops | about ____ scoops |
| 3. paper cup | about ____ scoops | about ____ scoops |

**Math Talk** Explain how you can tell which of the containers on this page is the largest.

# On Your Own

How many scoops does the container hold?
Estimate. Then measure.

| Container | Estimate | Measure |
|---|---|---|
| 4. jar | about ___ scoops | about ___ scoops |
| 5. milk carton | about ___ scoops | about ___ scoops |
| 6. bowl | about ___ scoops | about ___ scoops |

# PROBLEM SOLVING REAL WORLD

Solve.

7. The red bowl holds 5 scoops of rice. The blue bowl holds twice as much rice as the red bowl. How many scoops of rice do the two bowls hold in all?

___ scoops in all

**TAKE HOME ACTIVITY** • Have your child use a paper cup to estimate how much various containers hold. Then check his or her estimate by measuring how much each container holds.

**Lesson 17**

Name _____

# Describe Measurement Data

**Essential Question** What measurement data can a line plot show?

## Model and Draw

A line plot shows data on a number line.

Each X on this line plot stands for the length of 1 desk.

Lengths of Our Desks in Inches

__12__ desks were measured.
Two desks are __24__ inches long.

The longest desk is __27__ inches long.
The shortest desk is __21__ inches long.

## Share and Show

Write 3 more sentences to describe what the line plot above shows.

1. _____
_____

2. _____
_____

3. _____
_____

 **Math Talk** Suppose you measured another desk. If the desk was 23 inches long, how could you show this on the line plot above?

**Getting Ready for Grade 3** two hundred ninety-seven **P297**

# On Your Own

**Lengths of Our Classroom Books in Inches**

Use the line plot to answer the questions.

4. How many books are 9 and 10 inches in length?

   _____ books

5. What is the difference in length between the shortest and longest book?

   _____ inches

Write another question you can answer by looking at the line plot. Answer your question.

6. Question _____
   _____
   Answer _____

# PROBLEM SOLVING

7. Look at the table to the right. It shows Tom's books and their lengths. Add the data for the books to the line plot at the top of the page.

| Book | Length |
|------|--------|
| Reading | 11 inches |
| Math | 12 inches |
| Spelling | 9 inches |

**TAKE HOME ACTIVITY** • Ask your child to explain how to read the line plot on this page.

P298 two hundred ninety-eight

Name _____

## ✓ Checkpoint

### Concepts and Skills

Write the time shown on the clock. Then write the time I hour before and I hour after.

1.

   I hour before _____

   I hour after _____

2.

   I hour before _____

   I hour after _____

←|————|————|————|————|————|————|————|→
2:00 P.M.  3:00 P.M.  4:00 P.M.  5:00 P.M.  6:00 P.M.  7:00 P.M.  8:00 P.M.

Use the time line above. Solve.

3. A movie begins at 2:00 P.M. It is over at 5:00 P.M. How long is the movie?

   _____ hours

4. Madison arrives at a friend's house at 3:00 P.M. She leaves at 7:00 P.M. How long does she stay?

   _____ hours

Getting Ready for Grade 3

Subtract to solve. Show your work.

5. Will arrives at the library at 1:15 P.M.
   He leaves at 1:50 P.M. How long is
   Will at the library?

   _____ minutes

6. Andrew begins reading at 3:20 P.M.
   He stops reading at 3:45 P.M.
   How long did Andrew read?

   _____ minutes

How many scoops does the container hold? Estimate. Then measure.

7.
   **plastic cup**

   Estimate: about _____ scoops

   Measure: about _____ scoops

8. What is the difference in height between the shortest and tallest plants?

**Heights of Plants in Inches**

○ 3 inches
○ 4 inches
○ 5 inches
○ 6 inches

Name _____

**Lesson 18**

# Fraction Models: Thirds and Sixths

**Essential Question** How can you identify thirds and sixths?

## Model and Draw

__3__ equal parts or __3__ thirds

__6__ equal parts or __6__ sixths

__1__ part of 3 equal parts or
__1__ third

__1__ part of 6 equal parts or
__1__ sixth

## Share and Show

Color the strips. Show two different ways to show 1 third.

1.  
2.  

Color the strips. Show two different ways to show 1 sixth.

3.  
4.  

**Math Talk** How are 3 thirds and 6 sixths alike?

Getting Ready for Grade 3

three hundred one **P301**

# On Your Own

Color the strips. Show two different ways to show 2 thirds.

5. 

6. 

Color the strips. Show two different ways to show 2 sixths.

7. 

8. 

Color the strips. Show two different ways to show 3 sixths.

9. 

10. 

# PROBLEM SOLVING REAL WORLD

Solve. Write or draw to explain.

11. A sub sandwich is cut into sixths. Tim eats two parts of the sandwich. How many parts are left?

_____ parts left

**TAKE HOME ACTIVITY** • Have your child draw a picture that shows a slice of cheese divided into thirds.

P302 three hundred two

Name _____

**Lesson 19**

# Fraction Models: Fourths and Eighths

**Essential Question** How can you identify **fourths** and **eighths**?

## Model and Draw

__4__ equal parts or __4__ fourths          __8__ equal parts or __8__ eighths

__1__ part of 4 equal parts or          __1__ part of 8 equal parts or
__1__ fourth                              __1__ eighth

## Share and Show

Color the strips. Show two different ways to show 1 fourth.

1.                                         2.

Color the strips. Show two different ways to show 1 eighth.

3.                                         4.

 **Math Talk**   How are 4 fourths and 8 eighths alike?

**Getting Ready for Grade 3**                    three hundred three **P303**

# On Your Own

**Color the strips. Show two different ways to show 2 fourths.**

5. 

6. 

**Color the strips. Show two different ways to show 3 eighths.**

7. 

8. 

**Color the strips. Show two different ways to show 5 eighths.**

9. 

10. 

## PROBLEM SOLVING REAL WORLD

Solve. Write or draw to explain.

11. A loaf of bread is cut into eighths. Jake uses 2 parts to make his lunch. Fran uses 3 parts to make her lunch. How many parts of the loaf are left?

_____ parts left

**TAKE HOME ACTIVITY** • Have your child draw a picture to show a slice of cheese divided into fourths.

Name _____

**Lesson 20**

## Compare Fraction Models

**Essential Question** How can you use fraction models to make comparisons?

### Model and Draw

| fourth | fourth | fourth | fourth |

| half | half |

1 fourth  <  1 half

### Share and Show

Color to show the fractions. Write <, =, or >.

1. 1 half | half | half |

   2 fourths | fourth | fourth | fourth | fourth |

   1 half ◯ 2 fourths

2. 1 fourth | fourth | fourth | fourth | fourth |

   1 eighth | eighth | eighth | eighth | eighth | eighth | eighth | eighth |

   1 fourth ◯ 1 eighth

**Math Talk** Look at the strips above. Is 1 half greater than or less than 3 fourths? How do you know?

**Getting Ready for Grade 3** three hundred five **P305**

# On Your Own

Color to show the fractions. Write <, =, or >.

3.  1 third | third | third | third |

   1 sixth | sixth | sixth | sixth | sixth | sixth | sixth |

   1 third ◯ 1 sixth

4.  3 sixths | sixth | sixth | sixth | sixth | sixth | sixth |

   1 half | half | half |

   3 sixths ◯ 1 half

# PROBLEM SOLVING REAL WORLD

Solve. Draw to show your answer.

5. Barry cut a cheese stick into halves and ate a half. Marcy cut a cheese stick into fourths and ate a fourth. Which child ate more cheese?

_____ ate more.

**TAKE HOME ACTIVITY** • Ask your child to draw a picture that shows a square divided into fourths.

P306 three hundred six

Name _____

# ✓ Checkpoint

## Concepts and Skills

Color the strips. Show two different ways to show 1 third.

1. 

2. 

Color the strips. Show two different ways to show 2 sixths.

3. 

4. 

Color the strips. Show two different ways to show 2 fourths.

5. 

6. 

Color the strips. Show two different ways to show 4 eighths.

7. 

8. 

**Getting Ready for Grade 3**   three hundred seven **P307**

Color to show the fractions. Write >, <, or =.

9. 1 half

| half | half |
|---|---|

3 fourths

| fourth | fourth | fourth | fourth |
|---|---|---|---|

1 half ◯ 3 fourths

10. 1 third

| third | third | third |
|---|---|---|

2 sixths

| sixth | sixth | sixth | sixth | sixth | sixth |
|---|---|---|---|---|---|

1 third ◯ 2 sixths

11. A pizza has 6 slices. Six friends share the pizza equally. What fraction of the pizza does each friend eat?

○ 1 third
○ 2 thirds
○ 1 sixth
○ 2 sixths

P308 three hundred eight